AUDACIOUS MINDSET

7 LIFE PRINCIPLES YOUNG WOMEN NEED TO THRIVE WITHOUT COMPROMISE

HEATHER HENDERSON

For more information, email audaciousmindset@gmail.com
ISBN: 978-0-578-83756-7

Cover design by 100Covers
Interior design by FormattedBooks

DEDICATION

My Dear Haydn,

You were born to be so much more than average. You are a leader. Only by taking risks can you fulfill your true potential. Take initiative and create your own opportunities. Be genuine and embrace your crazy. Stay strong and persistent, and you will achieve all you desire. You, my dear, have an audacious mindset!

My Darling Beeje,

You live your life by your own set of rules, unafraid of how others perceive you. You are confident, kind, and carefree. Let your passion work for you, never against you. Continue to be your authentic self, and you will inadvertently attract whatever you desire. You, my darling, have an audacious mindset!

TABLE OF CONTENTS

INTRODUCTION

The word audacious is interesting as it takes on two vastly different and opposite meanings. The one is positive and the other negative. It is controversial and up for interpretation.

To me, the meaning of the word is quite positive, since being audacious requires you to be bold and fearless and have courage and persistence. You must be unafraid of criticism or adversity.

The negative connotation of this word refers to how others perceive you. If someone calls you audacious in the negative sense, they think you are reckless and insolent. However, at the end of the day, the only person's happiness you can control is your own; therefore, your opinion is the only one that matters. Choose to be audacious.

To be audacious, you must break convention and take actions the average person cannot fathom.

So often, too many people get sucked in by the comfort of their daily routines and status quo that they never give themselves the chance to take the readily available opportunities that could dramatically improve their lives. They cling to fear and self-sabotage rather than belief and faith. Fear is what traps us, not our circumstances.

People imagine everything that could go wrong instead of everything that can go right. Why is that? Why are we more content with the familiar than the unexpected? Why are we satisfied with routine and comfort rather than excitement and opportunity? The second likely proposes more work and more struggle with no guarantees, which makes us extremely uncomfortable.

We panic and cling to less-than-ideal situations because we fear an unknown alternative.

But let's be audacious—adventurous and bold. Let's dare to cross into the unknown.

Throughout the book, I will discuss several qualities and skills to create an audacious mindset. Some of these skills came naturally for me, and others I developed from lessons I learned.

As I share some painful and embarrassing stories, you will learn about the adversity and obstacles I have, and continue to struggle with, so you can succeed on your own journey. I want to encourage you to make small changes and choices that can positively impact the course of your life.

I live my life with no regrets and feel grateful and blessed for everything in my past and future. I am proof that your beginning does not have to be your ending. It does not define you. It is quite the opposite. You can use your struggles and stumbling blocks to build a life that far exceeds your expectations.

As a little girl, I felt lost and alone as I didn't grow up with a strong female role model. No female guided me and showed me how to step up and take control of situations. I had to lead and believe in myself. And it was far from pretty. I often found myself in bad situations because of my careless behavior. However, I was able to grow and learn a lot from my mistakes.

I know nowadays, women rule the world, and the sky is the limit. You constantly hear about women breaking glass ceilings and the endless opportunities they have, but those stories were never told to me. Instead, my mind was filled with negativity, doubt, and limitations. How could I be or achieve anything when I felt like I was nothing, except maybe a mistake.

As odd as it may sound, even though I may have been told I could not, I always clung to the hope that the restrictions imposed on me were not real.

Hope, faith, and a strong conviction helped me in my youth and continuously help guide me today. These characteristics are a few of the qualities that comprise an audacious mindset.

You must take hold of the power you possess. Once I let go of feeling sorry for myself and released the victimhood mentality, recognizing that I, in fact, held all the power in determining my failures and success, my life took a completely different turn. It sounds so simple, but if it were easy, then everyone would turn around their circumstances; but they do not.

My life was far from perfect, but I managed to take my hardships and learn lessons to not just accept the circumstances and a life given to me, but to create and cultivate a life I wanted to have.

We all have shitty things that happen to us, which we cannot control. It is our response and choices that can take us past tragedies into triumphs. This all starts with certain attributes; the attributes of an audacious mindset, which will be detailed throughout this book.

An audacious mindset, of course, begins with the individual. It is necessary to fix, build, and retrain your inner workings before you can expect any outer workings to produce anticipated results.

The qualities of an audacious mindset involve constant work and development as you must implement and practice them. But it is well worth the effort as the outside world around us becomes more beautiful when we find peace, balance, and acceptance internally.

An audacious mindset does not just happen without intention. It must be created if you seek improvement.

Once you start building the necessary skills and qualities, you will notice that an audacious mindset will never settle and, therefore, you cannot either. That does not mean you will not be satisfied, but it does mean that your growth and potential far exceed anything you could possibly imagine.

If you desire a more meaningful, positive, and fulfilling life that you are completely capable of constructing, then an audacious mindset is required.

If you start developing these qualities within yourself, that are outlined in the chapters of this book, your life will improve rapidly and dramatically. You will achieve the greatness you desire.

HUMBLE BEGINNINGS

"You are confined by the boundaries you set yourself.
The mind creates the cage. Set yourself free and
move out of your comfort zone." —Mhar

Before we go any further, I want you to know me and my story. Everything in this book, as well as my evolution, will make more sense if you know my background.

While I am not one to dwell on a negative past, we do need to come to peace with it and accept it. It does serve a purpose as it's a tool to learn and grow from. My outlook reflecting back on my past is one of gratitude. It built me exactly as I needed to be. I am so thankful.

Adversity and obstacles are sent your way for a reason. They build and shape you with a purpose. Take initiative and use your experiences as lessons to learn who exactly it is you are meant to be.

My family only consisted of my mother and father and me.

My early childhood was spent in a duplex in the ghetto. The neighborhood was bad, and the crime was growing. My house was broken into even though we lived right across the street from the police station.

Luckily, my dad came back home that night and was able to protect my mom and I from the intruder with his shotgun. Otherwise, it's hard to guess what would have happened. The intruder was never caught, so it left a very uneasy feeling. We eventually moved.

We were not economically stable by any means. We barely made ends meet. On top of the struggles poverty brings, my father was an alcoholic who was very abusive to my mother. I remember hiding under the chair with my hands covering my ears, hoping it all would stop soon.

My mother left us both, when I was eleven, for a new life with her boyfriend and drugs. She was in and out of the picture. When she was around, she was mentally abusive to me in ways that damaged my self-esteem and self-worth. I do not think she could even comprehend the damage she caused, nor do I believe those were her intentions.

She never believed in me, her expectations were very low, and I was always a disappointment in her eyes. She always told me I was just like my dad, so in a way, I think she could not stand me.

My dad was good to me, but he was on the road all the time for his job, so my primary caretaker was myself. Over the years, I stayed with friends, aunts, an older cousin, my dad's girlfriend at one point, and really anyone who would take me. I hung out in the projects and was hardly "home." I had little parenting and even less supervision. I was reckless.

I endured bullies, constant harassment, and got in several fights. As a result, I was suspended from school. The very same school where we had to wait outside so we could be shuffled like cattle through the metal detectors daily.

My recklessness didn't stop there. I was busted for shoplifting on several occasions, was arrested and charged with assault, and had a felony record by the time I was eighteen years old.

Because of this, no colleges wanted to accept me. Eventually, a community college accepted me, but I failed out of it.

I was so angry and resentful. I had a very dim future until I started making positive changes to impact my life. I assumed my power and responsibility and took control and ownership of my circumstances.

MY LIFE NOW

My life is vastly different from the one I left seventeen years ago. I rebuilt myself. Some things happened by "luck"; the rest was intentional. I went from being raised in a low-income household to becoming a top 4 percent individual income earner throughout the entire US. The best part is, I am part time.

I went from an academic failure that no college wanted to a highly sought-after entrepreneur that runs her own company. I am one of the few in my extended family that ever graduated college.

Now, in my mid-thirties, I live in a small town in West Virginia where they say opportunity is limited, yet we are the millionaires next door. I can proudly tell you that my greatest accomplishments are my happy and successful marriage to the love of my life, and my beautiful, amazing children.

I have an awesome inner circle and support system. My life is everything I have ever wanted.

I tell you all of this because if the broken little girl with a dim future could pick herself up, break the cycle, and go on and achieve greatness, I have not one ounce of doubt that you can too.

FINDING YOUR SUCCESS

I am aware, and will be the first to tell you, that success is far from limited to just financial earnings and wealth.

Success means different things to different people. What success means to you will likely change or vary throughout your lifetime; but success, no matter what it looks like or how you define it, will always begin with you.

You must achieve internal victories before you can achieve external victories. External results are the results of long and diligent internal working.

These internal victories come from having an audacious attitude. Just as you must believe in yourself, you have to trust in your circumstances.

Yes, it will be hard at first. You will likely experience struggles daily until, suddenly, something magical happens. At that point, your momentum will keep building, like a ball rolling down a hill.

Things will start going right; yes, you will encounter setbacks, but you will not get deterred because your mindset has shifted, you have developed good habits, and you are laser-focused on the end result.

This type of mentality is not for the timid. It will not exist for those who give up too easily. It is for those who are warriors and those that can endure pain and disappointment.

Although it will not be easy or expedient, if you are relentless you will succeed.

Before long, you will start achieving everything you could have ever imagined, and even better, things you have not.

1

THE SEVEN WORDS THAT CHANGED EVERYTHING

"We are born in one day. We die in one day. We can change in one day. And we can fall in love in one day. Anything can happen in just one day."—Gayle Forman

Shortly after my husband, Beau, and I met, my life changed with one simple question he asked: "What are you doing with your life?"

I did not know; I did not know how to answer it. I think my exact response was, "I'm not sure." I felt offended and embarrassed. Who was he to ask me what I was doing with my life? Of course, that was typical me with a chip on my shoulder, my what's-it-to-you attitude. But it touched a much deeper place in me where I was aggressively shaken awake.

The truth was that I never really thought about it. I was wandering and drifting through life to see where it would take me rather than living life with purpose or meaning. I did not want to face reality because I was scared. I did not know it at the time, but fear of the unknown kept me running from and avoiding all responsibility.

When I was a kid, I couldn't wait to grow up and take control of my life; and here I was feeling like I was too young to start living a life where I could actually be accountable for my choices. Also, I had absolutely no plan for my life, no vision, no goals—other than to be perfectly content in my current situation.

I liked to have fun, and I was very spontaneous and free-spirited. I did not take things too seriously, and I was really enjoying my life, living each day to the fullest. Or so I thought.

I understand why I was attractive to many; I was like a young butterfly—wild and free. While many liked the chase, others were completely scared off by the unpredictability. Beau loved everything I was and never wanted to change me. He just wanted to understand me. I was complicated and challenged him in a way which intrigued him.

The question, "what are you doing with your life," was so real because I realized in that moment, that just because I was good for the time being, that type of happiness would not last. It was in that moment I realized I had a lot to offer and that I was capable of so much more than what I was doing.

While my first try at college was met with rejection and failure, I decided to go back to school. This time was going to be different because I was ready, and I wanted change. I had spent enough time running from reality that I was failing on several levels, and it was time to act and face it all head-on.

I believed that school would be the initial change I had to take to start moving my life in a better direction. In my mind, this was my last chance. It was do or die.

This moment in my life changed the course of my thinking. Since this moment, my mentality shifted, and I did not give myself any other alternatives, excuses, or gray areas.

To compare it to science class and learning the states of matter, I underwent a chemical change. A chemical change is where you cannot physically change back the state into the original matter. It is permanently changed and altered. Once you start altering the state, you cannot reverse it. This was my transformation.

Before I met Beau, I was developing the habit of self-sabotage. My belief in myself and my capabilities was dwindling. Although no one would have known it, I wore my mask quite well.

I put off pursuing the great things I really wanted out of my life. I had no ambition, and I was caving into self-doubt. Beau did not see that at all. He saw something in me that I did not yet see myself.

He was so supportive the entire time. He was just starting his career, fresh out of college, and very hungry. He was ready to set the world on fire, and I was still trying to get the wheels on my car to enter the race.

He was not only supportive every step of the way, but he also set a wonderful example of what I could look forward to with life. Through his example, I learned how a hard work ethic could lead to great results. He was my mentor and my role model.

Some will say how lucky I was to have a Prince Charming come to my rescue. In which I reply, he was the angel sent to me that handed me the mirror so I could rescue myself.

CHAPTER APPLICATION

It is important to have a mentor or a role model. Ultimately, it lies within you to make a conscious choice, decision, and effort to start shaping your life in the way you want it.

We all have defining moments where our mentality shifts or a lightbulb moment where we decide to turn things around or to take a leap and forge ahead. A change will happen within you when you realize that you want and deserve more for your life.

1) Examine any or every aspect of your life. What is most important? What is suffering? Is it love, career, finances, education, family, health, or spirituality?

2) Are you content? What's missing? What could be better that would make you happier?

3) What can you improve? How can you improve? What changes can and do you need to make?

4) Determine your *WHY*. Once you determine your reasoning for *WHY* changes need to be made, it will be much easier to make and stay committed to those changes.

MASTERING YOUR MIND AND SETTING YOUR VISION

"How high you fly is derived from how big you think."—Robin Sharma

So often we hear how important it is to take time for yourself and how often women don't do that. Women seem to struggle with tremendous guilt if they worry or take time for themselves instead of others.

Luckily, I've never really had that struggle because my experience taught me that if we cannot take care of ourselves, who else will?

I realize as I have gotten older, had children, and assumed more responsibility, that time is an asset we have too little of. However, perhaps selfishly, I have always made myself a priority.

Because I often spent so much time alone growing up, I recognized the value and importance of taking care of myself and my needs. Since I was so used to being alone, now it is something I really require. But really, it is something everyone needs. The truth is, finding your strength and power is a self-centered process. You must make the time.

We all yearn to have happiness, harmony, and fulfillment, and that starts within. When you continue to grow and improve yourself, your relationships, your career, your spirituality, and more, then you can start to build a successful, happy life you can be satisfied with.

My life was never as blessed and balanced until I did some serious soul searching. I do it periodically because we evolve and change. When we really begin to explore ourselves on a deeper level, we can truly discover ourselves. Taking care of yourself includes time for reflection, as we have much to discover in our own thoughts and reflection.

Your outer world is often a reflection of your inner world. You need to achieve peace and order from within, then magically, the chaos that seemed to be closing in on you from the outside will disappear. Your circumstances will improve.

Our mind is the most powerful tool we own, and it shapes our way of life. It is our internal barriers, our self-limiting beliefs, that hold us back. The power we need to hold control over is our mind. As you go through this section, you will discover the ways you are currently treating yourself. What is your attitude toward yourself? What expectations do you have, and how forgiving are you of your mistakes? Do you have a vision on what you want for your life? Have you created goals and habits that align with the achievement of that vision?

If your vision is a masterpiece, then you are the artist; and your mindset, behaviors, goals, and habits are the canvas, paintbrushes, colors, technique, and application.

A vision, coupled with the right attitude, habits, goals, and pure determination can make all the difference within you to transform your circumstances and life.

These next three sections are crucial because self-love, self-respect, and self-trust are the foundations of an audacious mindset. If you cannot excel with these three concepts, you will always undermine yourself and be the greatest risk to your own progress. You will never reach your potential if do not do the following:

1) Believe in yourself.
2) Believe that what you want is out there and for you to have.

As the brilliant sentiment often attributed to David Brooks goes, "Almost every successful person begins with two beliefs: the future can be better than the present, and I have the power to make it so."

You are going to struggle at times. Your belief in yourself may come and go, but it is essential that you always find it, develop it, and continuously build upon it. Only then can you really maximize opportunities and live your life with intention.

2

MINDSET

"The only person you are destined to become is the person you decide to be."—Ralph Waldo Emerson

WHAT STORY ARE YOU TELLING YOURSELF?

Have you ever noticed how children are just naturally confident? I mean, before the world can interfere and lace their thoughts with self-doubt.

Toddlers are a prime example of this. They wear what they want, say what they want, and do and act exactly as they want. They push boundaries and limits because they do and think what feels good to them, and they see nothing wrong with it. They have no fear, and why would they? This is just a world of possibilities. They are like little explorers and adventurers that may ask *why* when they are told no, but what they really mean is *why not?*

It gets more complicated as we get older, when other people's judgments are bestowed upon us. We start caving into traditionalism or conventionalism to avoid conflict. What society and our peers tell us makes us second-guess how we behave and how we act.

A child's innocence is really a thing of beauty because in most cases, life experiences have not yet told them about limitations, dangers, and risks. All the things that so often hold us back as adults.

As we go through life, we adopt beliefs, habits, and a history that are all hard to change. But we must change them if they are not serving our best purpose. If they are limiting and obstructing us in any way, we must make changes.

You must retrain yourself, with a clean slate, to have an audacious mind. You must break past the internal barriers and limiting boxes you have put yourself in. It will be an uphill battle as you have to essentially defy gravity and go against the story you have accepted as the truth.

It is not about who you were or who you are, it is about who you need to become to fulfill the vision you have for your life.

When you can start constructing thoughts and actions that contribute to your overall improvement as a person, you will then continue to build on your hope and happiness. You will start to achieve little victories. You will begin to see a glimpse of your potential, and you will realize that you are so much more capable than you originally thought possible.

Remember, you are the artist of your life. It will be up to you what you create. You must know that it is never too late to create a beautiful masterpiece.

ATTITUDE

Because your thoughts and actions are dictated by the attitude you choose, your attitude is so important in all aspects of your life, especially how you view yourself and the world around you. Your attitude is the single greatest influence you have on yourself.

A bad attitude will jeopardize your relationship with others and yourself, threatening your progress, goals, and overall vision. It will literally make or break you.

Understand your attitude is not permanent; therefore, you create it. You can choose to have any attitude you desire. Is your current attitude producing success or defeat?

Life is obviously not fair, but how will you handle your challenges? Will you respond with more defeating behaviors or with a new sense of hope and eagerness to try a different approach? Your reactions will stem from the attitude you hold.

Your attitude is the energy you exude, so what message are you communicating? Are you bitter, resentful, and just flat-out miserable to be around? Or do you carry a light within you that makes other's experiences with you pleasurable?

Did you ever notice that people can just choose to be in a bad mood for no reason whatsoever? So, then they could choose to be enthusiastic, happy, and grateful without any reason either. That type of positive attitude about life will help you excel and enjoy it the most.

Pessimistic vs. Optimistic

A negative attitude toward yourself will do absolutely nothing to contribute to your success. If you are pessimistic, all your thoughts and actions will be guided by negativity. You will have no initiative because you will be consumed by doubt and fear, always feeling defeated rather than empowered.

A pessimistic outlook will persuade you against any type of action. You will find a million reasons why you should not and every excuse possible to back up your reasons. Whether it's self-doubt, fear, or a resistance to change, you are limiting your potential. Whatever justification or reasoning you have, it is nothing more than an excuse. Any excuse you have is not good enough for not living with the happiness you can achieve.

Is there an annoying, devilish critic in your mind hell-bent on filling your mind with negative thoughts? How often do you have negative thoughts about yourself? *Gosh, why did I say that? I sounded so stupid! I look so gross today! I hate my hair! I will never get it right! I am stuck. I don't know why I bother; it never works out. I am too old to change XYZ.* The list goes on. You get the point.

Are any of your good thoughts diminished by the critic?

What do you think that does to your self-esteem? Of course, it absolutely tears you apart. These are simply self-limiting beliefs that are not honest because they are not the entire truth.

Whether they have been instilled into you from others with self-defeating beliefs or your own past experiences, these stories are based on perception, not reality, and regardless, can always be rewritten.

At any given time, you can rewrite your reality.

Tip #1: To do that, follow Annie Grace's ACT technique explained in her book, *The Alcohol Experiment*. It is an amazing way to shift your mind and perspective. It stands for awareness, clarity, and turnaround. You first have to identify the belief, explore why you're accepting it as the truth, and then turn around the belief. You reject the original, negative belief by finding supporting reasons that it has no validation. When you start exploring and influencing your thoughts, your behaviors will change.

You can do this with any and every insecurity, uncertainty, or situation you may have in your own life.

I am in the sales game, which can be a brutal and mentally exhausting sport. So, I have used the ACT technique to overcome my fears when calling on prospective clients:

1) Awareness (belief): I am likely to have a negative experience met with rejection and failure.

2) Clarity (why the belief): Sales is a numbers game and no matter my approach, seven out of ten times, I will be turned down. This is based on my past experiences. Excessive rejection results in disappointment and self-doubt. However, rejection isn't necessarily negative. What can I learn? I can learn what to do better on my next call if I don't get this sale. I can have fun with a new, outrageous approach. I can practice and perfect my technique. What new people can I encounter and experience? By not trying, isn't it also negative because I don't get the sale? I may fail, but I fail anyway if I don't try.

3) Turnaround (replace the belief): There is nothing more rewarding than overcoming challenges to gain a new client. This could be a great client who needs my help. I can save them a lot of money and build a great working relationship. They may like my approach and refer me to a friend. I am a trusted advisor and an expert in my field. This is their lucky day.

If you don't learn how to control and train your mind to be stronger than your impulses, you will inadvertently destroy everything you are working toward. Turn around your insecurities and doubts and replace them with liberating truths.

Following the ACT technique consistently will give you an optimistic attitude about yourself and your situations. Optimism breeds hope and will ultimately help you believe that the vision you have for yourself and your future can become reality.

Optimism is what will keep you going when times get tough, and you want to quit on the goals you set for yourself. Optimism is what will motivate you to act because you are convinced that with that action, you will achieve your desired outcome. You know in your heart that although the results of your daily actions may not be expedient, they will pay off and lead to much greater rewards in the bigger picture.

Tip #2: Along with the ACT technique, you can also direct your efforts toward actions and not so much on your thoughts. That way you do not get caught up and miss your purpose.

For example, when I am about to walk in to try and gain the business of a new client, my nerves can get the best of me. My mind races with thoughts such as, *I shouldn't go in. They are probably going to be busy and hostile toward my interruption. What if I mess up what I want to say? I don't want to deal with the conflict and rejection.* I shut it all down quickly by literally physically forcing myself out of the car. I force myself into action, and I am always relieved when I do. The outcome is always better than the assumptions I imagine.

Tip #3: Focus on gratitude and switch negative thoughts to positive. When I have a bad day, and start thinking about everything bad that happened and begin to relive it, I immediately flip the switch to gratitude so I can remind myself about how fortunate I really am.

I also remind myself that I am a work in progress, and I am growing and improving every day. You must really switch out your negative thoughts into positive, helpful, productive ones. You have to change up your thinking about not only yourself but your situation. As the quote credited to Wayne Dyer states, "If you believe it will work out, you'll see opportunities. If you believe it won't, you will see obstacles."

If you do not yet have one, make a gratitude list daily so you are aware of how blessed you truly are. This simple practice can positively alter your state of mind. We will get more into gratitude and affirmations and their importance in chapter 21.

If you are, in fact, having a terrible day, it can be very difficult to pull yourself out of the weeds to get some clarity to actually put your life in perspective; but you have to because if you don't, those negative thoughts and ideas will spread like a wildfire.

Remember this always; you are in control. You are in control of your actions and most certainly your thoughts.

EXPECTATIONS

We all demand things from ourselves and often get very frustrated, angry, and so quick to attack ourselves when we cannot meet the expectations, we set for ourselves—even when the expectations are improper. This extra stress we put on ourselves often contributes to more negative thoughts, actions, and self-doubt.

Expectations can be properly managed when they are aligned with goals. Expectations are the hope you have for an outcome, but goals are, in part, the process to achieve your expectations. Your goals will be based on intention and action.

While you may not be able to control the outcome of your expectations, goals give you your best shot at bringing about your desired outcome.

It is important to set challenging, but realistic goals. You need to stretch, but not pull apart.

Before you even set goals, you need to:

1) Assess your current situation.
2) Acknowledge your weaknesses and potential challenges to better confront these.
3) Commit to the end result.
4) Remember that your expectations should not devalue the experience.

For example, let's take two people who set the goal of becoming healthier this year. They hear about their local sprint triathlon in thirty days and consider participating to contribute to their goal.

The one is in good physical shape, exercises regularly, and eats pretty healthy daily. The other person is overweight, hasn't exercised since college, and eating healthy consists of diet coke.

Who do you think has a more realistic chance of sticking to and achieving their goal of completing the sprint triathlon?

A more realistic goal for the second individual would be to train for the community 10k that takes place in three months.

Regardless of whether it is a sprint triathlon or a 10k, both are valuable experiences that will provide an individual with discipline and lessons that can be helpful later. Each event, while different, contribute to an individual's goal of becoming healthier.

We need to responsibly manage our goals and our expectations because they will shape our actions and perceptions. It is all about progress, even baby steps. It is about improving, growing, and moving closer toward our overall vision.

FORGIVENESS

You will screw up and make mistakes along the way, and that is okay. Just like we should be quick to forgive a young child who makes a mistake, we should be delicate with ourselves in a similar manner. We, too, are growing and learning, so compassion from ourselves is so important. As Confucius said, "Our greatest glory is not in never falling, but in rising every time we fall."[1]

We are not, and we will never be, perfect; but we must learn from our mistakes. When we can look at situations as learning experiences rather than failures, we do ourselves a lot more good than harm.

It is important to not let the things we have no control over discourage us. Our goals can ensure we do all the right things leading up to the end result, trying to guarantee our desired outcome, but some things are out of our control.

Expectations can be beneficial but use them with caution. Expectations should not create an emotional attachment that interferes with your happiness. Just because you anticipate a certain outcome, doesn't mean you can't find the silver lining in unforeseen circumstances. There are positive aspects in every outcome. Have an open mind and an open heart.

We have to allow for flexibility and room for unexpected changes. If we are too rigid, we can cause ourselves more disappointment and conflicts. We should learn to enjoy the surprises along the way because it is likely they are profound blessings on our journey.

We must recognize this and allow forgiveness of ourselves and our circumstances, in order to try again and again, until we reach our goals. A person is not a failure who attempts and fails. It is often our failings that lead to our success; if we don't give up too soon.

An optimistic attitude, proper expectations and goals, coupled with forgiveness, will give you the motivation and resilience to keep striving forward.

CHAPTER APPLICATION

What insecurities, limiting beliefs, and negative thoughts are preventing you from achieving the expectations, goals, and potential you have in your own life? Take the time, make a list writing them all down, and really explore them. Do it before you move on.

Once you have identified those negative thoughts and ideas with pen and paper, I want you to counterattack the negative thought for a liberating truth. Your liberating truth is a positive and optimistic belief.

For example, "I'm terrible at relationships and probably will be single for the rest of my life," is not honest, but it may be a belief you have. The truth is, you learned from past relationships what you do and you do not want. You are lovable, kind, and desirable. When you meet the right person, it will all work out because you want and deserve love.

Do this exercise for every, single, negative belief that enters your mind and attempts to sabotage you. Do it as often as necessary. Recognition and replacement are key.

It is like the phrase coined by Brandeis, "sunlight is said to be the best of disinfectants."[2] Your negative thoughts are like germs that you must discover and disinfect by exposing them. This transparency will allow your liberating truths to guide you. When you start applying your optimistic outlook as the new truth, you can shape a better reality.

So many of us need proof and must see to believe. But what if I told you that only when you begin to believe is when you can actually see?

3

GAME PLAN

"Setting goals is the first step in turning the invisible into the visible."—Tony Robbins

The previous chapter was about developing techniques to overcome the limitations and barriers in your mind. These next two chapters are about how to love yourself by taking the time to care for yourself. Self-care involves doing all you can to feel the best about yourself.

The activities you do to make yourself happy will vary depending on the person, but I have found there are three elements of my being that I really have to focus on in order to feel my best. More to come on those in the following chapter.

You can find many ways to recharge yourself and feel better. Getting your hair done, a massage, or even a pedicure are all acts of self-care that can make you feel good. However, these things, as nice as they are, are temporary and fleeting forms of happiness as self-care.

I want to take you on a deeper level of self-exploration to discover your wants, your passions, your vision, and how to achieve all you desire. These will be the ultimate acts of self-love and self-care.

VISION

A grand vision will require you to raise the expectations you have for yourself. The vision you have for your life is often deeper and more aligned with your character and purpose for being.

You need to visualize what you really want in your life. The vision you set for yourself should include your strongest wants and hopes for your future. Each piece must be clear. Clarity is key for achieving your vision.

Your vision should permeate such enthusiasm that it carries you beyond any of your previous expectations or limits you've imposed on yourself. It will motivate and inspire you in such a way that you are compelled to move beyond your familiarity.

I cannot stress this part enough; a *wish* and a *want* are different. You need to focus on your wants.

The strongest wants I have created for myself over the years have taken on the form of a need. I make them nonnegotiable and essential. A *want* is a more precise focus and takes on decisive action.

When you have a strong, clear vision for your life, your *wants* will drive you to become the person necessary to help you reach your desire.

Part of the process to obtain your vision will require you to learn, grow, and progress. As you follow your vision, an evolution within yourself will take place, and you will surpass the barriers in your mind to access infinite possibilities. Your vision will derive from your values.

VALUES

"It's not hard to make decisions when you know what your values are."—Roy Disney

A vision is much easier to create by first identifying the values most important to you. I strongly suggest you take the time to write down and explore your own values. Your top seven, then five, then three. These values will be your guiding force. Your values determine your character, and your character represents your authentic self.

Here are a few examples of some values that may be important in your own life:

Achievement	Compassion	Family
Balance	Creativity	Freedom
Bravery	Fairness	God

Growth	Justice	Recognition
Health	Leadership	Service
Honesty	Loyalty	Simplicity
Improvement	Love	Wealth
Integrity	Kindness	
Independence	Power	

The list goes on. Once you identify your own values, you can begin to get clarity on your own decisions and actions. Your values and morals will motivate you and be your inner compass throughout your life. Your specific values need to be upheld with boundaries, discipline, and accountability.

Creating the vision

After witnessing my own mother's struggles, I never wanted to feel as though I was stuck in a situation or in a relationship that was not of my choosing. So, I created the vision of becoming a successful businesswoman to grant me access to things I value, such as, freedom, financial independence, and achievement.

Once I achieved that vision, I made a vision for my business. I operate my business with the values of integrity and honesty at the center and believe it is what gives me a competitive advantage. I will not lie and practice unethical standards that has, sadly, been common practice in my industry in an effort to get ahead. I am very fair and follow the golden rule that states, "treat others the way you wish to be treated."

My business allows me to have the freedom to focus on another high-priority value, my family. I created the vision to have strong bonds as a partner and a parent. I want to be supportive and loving in any and every possible way. Great relationships with my husband and children are my most important priority.

GOALS

Goals help you to achieve your overall vision. They encompass many facets with specific ideas, strategies, and actions to align you with your overall vision. Your vision can be composed of long-term habit goals and short-term achievement goals that correlate with your values. Your goals should excite and even scare you.

After coming up with a list of your goals, you need to keep them in the forefront of your mind. Goals are not to be made and then forgotten; they are to be reviewed and adjusted accordingly.

I like to review the goals I set for myself monthly. It is a good time to reflect on how far I've come, the areas in which I need to improve, and a plan going forward to correct my actions to move me closer to any long-term goal or vision I have.

Let me be very blunt. Goal setting is what separates winners from losers. If you do not have a vision and goals to get you to that vision, do you really have a purpose?

Your goals should follow the famous S.M.A.R.T. acronym. They should be specific, measurable, achievable, relevant, and timely. Look up this concept, if you are not familiar, to help you with your goal setting.

To achieve my vision of teaching my children strong values, I made a goal to write this book. But the goal was not simply, *I will write a book this year.* I had to really break it down, plan, and execute it for it to become reality.

I like planning and determining success by numbers because it's very black and white for me.

For example, in order to write this book, I knew I needed around 40,000 words. I knew that I would have roughly twenty-six chapters. So, I would need each chapter to be roughly 1,600 words.

I also knew that I wanted to finish my book within three months, or ninety days, roughly. Thus, I would need to write about 450 words daily to stay on course consistently and to stay motivated. That meant I needed to write roughly two chapters a week.

Notice that once I determined the goal, I developed a specific time frame in which to complete the goal. From that point, I determined which habits and actions I would have to commit to daily to achieve this goal. Once I planned all the details, the only thing left to do was to act.

Do you see how much easier something that was once overwhelming can be broken down and broken down, step-by-step, until you have a manageable, daily game plan and course of action?

I do this with every aspect of my life from my career, new clients, finances, family, health, personal life, and education. It is so easy to get overwhelmed and bogged down unless you take it step-by-step.

I suggest you grab a planner to really track your results. There are so many planners out there that can help you create a vision, track your goals, and master habits in every aspect of your life. Your planner should act as your motivation and hold you accountable.

CHAPTER APPLICATION

Your vision should align with your values. Your vision will create the why and purpose of your goals. Your vision will act almost as the destination, and your goals will map out the direction you take as well as the stops and progress of your journey to reach that destination. So, you want to take three steps:

1) Determine the values essential to you.
2) Construct a vision that encompasses your values.
3) Formulate goals that will help you achieve your vision(s).

If you take the time to create goals and write them down, plan, and execute them, you will recognize their importance. For they are what allow you to maximize your potential. Once you start to get a glimpse of what you are capable of, you start to believe in yourself. When you believe in yourself, you find it easier to love and trust yourself. Therefore, goals are a critical component in building on the foundation for self-love.

Your values, visions, and goals are vital to your future. Get clarity on these three components. Make time for this process.

4

EXECUTE

*"There are no limits. There are only plateaus, and you must
not stay there, you must go beyond them."—Bruce Lee*

Have you gotten the sense that my form of self-care requires hard work? Well, it does; a lot. The self-care I want you to achieve will not be obtained in a salon. It will require you to push yourself as a way to care for yourself. It is that tough love that we all need.

The three elements I mentioned previously that are essential for you to care for are your physical, mental, and spiritual being. P.M.S., the kind you should embrace. It is important to nourish these three elements of your life daily to achieve balance and contentment. Since they are closely intertwined, when all three are activated and engaged to start your day, you will produce the best results and have the most fulfilling days. Personal development routines will transform you into the person you need to be in order to obtain the life you want to live. These routines are present throughout my habits by design.

Habits are things you do every day; therefore, they become a part of who you are, your character. They coincide with your goals, and, in fact, are the acts that ensure you achieve your goals.

Good habits can only be developed, initially, through strong self-discipline. You must be in control of yourself and your time. How well you manage your time will be the determining factor for how successful you will be.

Effectively managing the time that we are all given daily, which is the same twenty-four hours, is what determines the outcome of your days, goals, and life.

To really contribute to your overall success, you have to be very disciplined with your habits. You must have a meaningful *why* to even start them, a solid commitment to stick with them, and accountability to make sure you are doing them consistently to get the results you desire.

You will have to develop and adjust them accordingly. They are the ultimate acts of self-care because completing them contributes to your overall well-being.

HABITS

Typically, whenever I come up with new goals, I know they will need to be supported by new habits. Habits are the routines we do on pretty much a subconscious level. We feel a strong need to complete our habits because not doing them feels utterly uncomfortable.

I am not referring to the mundane habits like brushing your teeth, buckling your seat belt, or even smoking, although they are habits, and they were developed. I am referencing the habits that you develop to contribute to certain goals you have.

I have fitness and nutrition goals for my physical well-being. I set continuous learning goals for my mental health. And to contribute to my spiritual side, I practice morning rituals.

I develop new habits as a strategy to fulfill my goals. The better the habits, the higher the probability of success for achieving your goals.

To form a habit, you need to repeat certain actions and behaviors consistently.

Habits may require work and struggle initially, but with enough repetition, you will easily tackle them.

To coincide with my vision for my health, I have a nutrition goal. I must eat healthy and supply myself with food that acts as fuel for my body. Since I know that time constraints can lead to less than desirable choices when it comes to what you eat, I have developed the habit of meal planning and doing as much food preparation as possible every Sunday.

It may take up most of the day, but I know I do not have any other time during the week to do it.

I have made getting up at 4:30 a.m. a habit because it allows me to complete my rituals and routines that are necessary in setting my mood and productivity for the day. This simple habit has tremendous impact on my other habits and goals. This simple habit has changed my whole life.

Not a morning person? Maybe that's just another limiting belief you've been fooling yourself with. Getting up earlier at first can be exceedingly difficult, however, this is the time you can consistently incorporate the three important elements essential to your care, well-being, and personal development.

Early morning is the time that I set aside for myself with no distractions (because the world is still comfy in their beds) to tap into my mental, physical, and spiritual sides.

I conduct my morning rituals. I meditate, read daily devotions, say my affirmations, and my prayers; and then I work out for the last thirty minutes. Sometimes, it is challenging to get it all in, but I know it sets the tone for the rest of my day.

I know how important exercise is to my overall vision for my health, and I have no other time to do it except first thing before everyone else in my house is up.

Do I love working out? No, of course not. I mean, I have better days than others, but I do not enjoy sweating. I do not enjoy being uncomfortable. I do not like struggling, shaking, and feeling like I can't breathe! (I have heard about the "runners high" and how it feels so good, but I cannot even imagine that because cardio is my least favorite.)

I exercise for no other reason besides the results. I love the results of being fit way more than I hate the act of getting fit. Of course, I like being in shape, but it's more than that. I like that I am committed. I show up, and when I am done, I feel a sense of pride.

I feel energized, renewed, and ready to take on whatever is going to come the rest of my day because I am totally in control. I feel like from then on, my day is proactive and not reactive. I am on offense instead of defense.

I like that when I exercise in the morning, my mind is sharper throughout the day. Just by completing my morning habits and rituals, I feel in total control and on fire. My mental and physical beings are so well connected that success of one is almost dependent on the other.

I recently developed the habit of the good old automobile university, a term coined by the late Zig Ziglar. I drive in a car for so much of my day that I figure I might as well put that time to good use. I make the most of my time by tapping into my mental psyche and increasing my knowledge. My Bluetooth is automatically picked up when I get into my car, so my audiobook just plays.

The right book can give you a new perspective or motivation to conquer your day. Therefore, I have made a habit out of listening to books just about every time I drive.

I also listen to an audio book while I'm getting ready rather than hearing the toxic news or mind-numbing shows. I want to feel enlightened when starting my day.

Just as easily as you can develop good habits, you can easily build on or break bad ones as well. They are formed based on intention and decisive action.

The point is, if you really want to start making some positive changes, you have to have a clear intention to dedicate and effectively manage your time in order to start reaping the rewards of even the smallest adjustments you make.

You do not have to do big things right away. I started off by simply drinking 16 oz. of water when I first woke up before I did anything else. I did this to rehydrate my body and increase my energy levels to kick-start my day.

Start small. Focus on just a few things. Do not overwhelm yourself to the point that you get discouraged. Build on the momentum. Once you have mastered one, you can move on to the next.

PROGRESS

Progress is so important, and I did not really understand how much so until I recently came across a Tony Robbins YouTube video sent to me by my friend. "Progress Equals Happiness." Well, you may wonder, like I did, *What does that mean exactly?*

As he started to explain it, I could relate so perfectly to it.

In pursuit of goals to achieve our vision, we will experience both victories and setbacks. All of these will be temporary. Yes, even great achievements do not create long-term happiness. They are just chapters in our books and mile markers along our journeys. However, progress is never-ending and what creates the satisfaction we really desire.

Progress is the choice we make to keep on going and pushing ourselves. It is how we hold ourselves accountable and keep stretching for just a little bit more. It is about frequently, expanding beyond our comfort zone.

I must be challenged and pushed to grow and excel. Only when I grow am I genuinely happy. I feel this is the same for every individual. If we are not moving closer to our goals and our vision, then we can only be moving away from them. In life, if we are stagnated, we cannot learn and improve, we cannot progress; therefore, we cannot be fulfilled.

Anytime you set goals, you set yourself up to grow and get better, regardless of the outcome, and you make progress toward your overall vision. Your progress impacts your character. This entire process is designed to have trials and help you build on your character.

Progress is about becoming who you need to be to graduate to the next rung of the ladder. There will always be a new level within your grasp; you just must keep looking up. So, once you have met all your goals and achieved your vision, you make a new vision and then new goals to help you achieve that vision. The love you have for yourself will strengthen when you hold yourself accountable to achieve your goals and make progress to fulfill your vision.

CHAPTER APPLICATION

In the last chapter, you created your game plan, a vision. Now it is time to execute it. If you haven't done so already, write down the goals you need to achieve to make your vision a reality. Next, write down the habits you will acquire to fulfill your goals. Your habits will help ensure that the goals you set are met. When your motivation and enthusiasm falter, these actions will keep you on track. Habits are the details that really put your plan into motion. Time is of the essence, so start developing better habits today.

Progress is about the journey, and who you become along the way, not the destination. You only must be better than you were yesterday. So, you should reflect once a month to track your progress. To do that, you need to write down everything. The more detailed the better. What have you improved, what still needs attention and more effort?

It's your personal preference as to what you use to help keep you on track and organized. However, organizational planners, such as the *InnerGuide* or the *Legend Planner,* have helped me tremendously along the way. They are much more than just appointment and schedule keepers. They will inspire you and really guide you every step of the way. These "planners" are really journals that act as a compass to discover or be the best version of yourself.

HONOR YOURSELF

"There will always be someone who can't see your worth. Don't let it be you."—Unknown

All the suggestions and strategies in the first section will help you build self-love; now, this section will discuss the ways in which you can uphold and honor that love. The two are complimentary. The more you learn to love yourself, the more value you will see, which allows you to respect yourself; and the more respect you gain for yourself, the more love you build for yourself.

Your self-respect is determined by the way you view your worth. You should know that you are deserving and are responsible to fulfill your own happiness. And because you now recognize the importance of your values and interests, you will protect them in order to protect your well-being.

Without self-respect, you cannot live the life you are meant to. When you respect yourself, you give yourself permission and access to achieve your vision. Self-respect impacts so many components of your life and your relationships; it influences just about every decision you will make, which is why it is so critical.

Gaining respect involves establishing boundaries, discipline, and accountability. It is the acceptance of yourself and honoring what you truly want. This authenticity will allow you to be true to yourself and others.

With respect, you will dismiss those who aren't deserving, and you will attract the right ones who will support and encourage you throughout your journey.

The love and respect you have toward yourself is crucial to your happiness.

5

SELF-RESPECT

"No man is free who is not a master of himself."—Epictetus

You must know what you are worthy of. When you respect yourself, you will not settle for less than what you deserve. This, at times, can require courage and audacity. The way you feel and act should represent honor and dignity.

Without self-respect, you will make other's needs your first priority. Caring for other's needs is important, but not when their needs always come at the expense of your own needs.

I'm not suggesting abandoning the needs of those you love, but I am telling you that if you get into the habit of constantly putting your own needs on the back burner, well, eventually, they get left there to burn.

Respecting yourself is about respecting your time, your needs, your goals, and your focus to do what is necessary to fulfill your desires.

When you feel lost, tired, or just not happy, it is directly related to not prioritizing yourself. When your quality of life is suffering, then you have sacrificed your self-respect.

Respect for yourself is obtained only by earning it. It will reflect choices you make and actions you take repeatedly.

BOUNDARIES

"You have enemies? Good. It means you stood up for yourself at one point."—Winston Churchill

In some regards, self-respect came very naturally to me. Fairness was always at the forefront of my mind, so I was never going to let someone get away with treating me poorly. After my mom left, I had a grudge against the world.

I am not saying it was right by any means, but it was a reason I set up boundaries, and perhaps even walls, around myself. I had to really look out for myself and protect myself. I always believed that if I did not, no one else was going to.

While my behavior toward myself at times did not always reflect self-respect, I did not tolerate other's disrespect for too long.

I remember watching a Dr. Phil episode a long time ago where he said, "You teach people how to treat you." People treat you the way you let them. It was a powerful message that carries with me years later. If you cannot love and respect yourself, why should others?

Far too often, there are examples of women in the unhealthiest relationships. I have witnessed myself, my mother, my friends, and even strangers accept less than what they deserve from a partner. Partner means equal. These women justify mistreatment as a sacrifice for someone they love. They make excuses instead of accepting the truth of their situations.

It's hard to respect yourself when you don't love yourself. If you do not love and respect yourself, then you cannot establish boundaries of acceptable behavior. Distinct boundaries reflect what behavior you are willing to tolerate. You will establish boundaries for both yourself and others. Once you set the boundaries, you set the foundation for that relationship.

In setting up your boundaries, remember the values you created.

You set up boundaries to ensure your values are being upheld. Your values should be protected and respected. Clear values will determine distinct boundaries that will build your self-respect.

Boundaries could be as simple as to not put yourself down in front of anyone, jokingly or not. *Oops, I'm such a ditz.*

Or they could be more complicated, like distancing yourself from a toxic friend or relative that drains you by constantly complaining about how terrible life is and how unfair the world is.

Maybe it's harder and requires you to tell your boss *NO,* and that you are not going to work overtime unless justly compensated.

It could be telling your client that you will not give them the discount they desire because your work and time is worth more than what they would like to pay.

If you don't stand up for yourself, then you are sacrificing your respect and happiness.

Here are some examples of boundaries you should establish and enforce:

1) Don't speak badly about anyone, including yourself.
2) Be direct, be assertive, and speak up in order to see that your needs are not being sacrificed.
3) Stop agreeing to everything. Learn how to say no. Your time is valuable; treat it as such.
4) Let go of feeling guilty and being ashamed. Stop being overly apologetic.
5) Look no further than yourself for validation. The most important approval you can seek will come from within.

WELCOME CONFLICTS

"You wouldn't let assholes live in your house. Why let them live in your head?"—Unknown

In setting boundaries, you need to be okay with conflict. When individuals are interfering with your peace of mind, the only way to resolve a conflict is to confront it. You must evict them from your mind to take back your peace.

Speak up to let them know their actions are not acceptable, and, therefore, they will not be tolerated. You can sit and stew, or you can act.

I never expected to have to deal with a recent situation, but, of course, it occurred in, of all places, church.

Have you ever been in a situation where someone is just a little too interested in your significant other? Well, this was it. I was caught off guard a little bit. But after numerous incidents, it became pretty obvious.

She was a volunteer; she greeted each person as they entered the chapel. So, the first time we were walking in together, she said, "Hi, Beau," and naturally, he said "hi" back. When we sat down at our seats, I was a little puzzled. Because of how she said it, long and drawn out, I asked him, "Who is that?" He replied, "I have no idea." I believed him, but I found the encounter odd.

The strange feeling in my gut was confirmed the following week. When my husband walked in with my children and I, you would have thought Ryan Reynolds had just walked in. She and her friend began whispering. The whispering, intense staring, giddiness, and giggles were quite embarrassing.

It was obvious she had a major crush and wanted his attention. I would catch her staring and hoping for an opportunity to say hi to him. It was shocking, as she acted as if I did not even exist.

I remember it got to the point where I was beyond irritated. Beau even admitted that he was uncomfortable. It was too much and crossing a line.

It was time to confront her and restore my peace. She was collecting donations at the end of the service when she thought it was necessary to say goodbye to my husband. I immediately said very calmly, "Hi, I'm Heather, his wife. Beau doesn't seem to remember you. How is it that you know him exactly?" She was extremely uncomfortable and awkward. I stood there with a smirk, intently interested in the answer she was going to give me.

She tried to explain that she babysat for one of his aunts at one point. She was telling me who her dad was and asking if I knew her dad, as if all these poor excuses were sufficient to act like she knew him well with blatant disregard and disrespect for his wife.

I just listened for about sixty seconds with genuine curiosity, looks of puzzlement, and condensation until I finally ended the conversation. "So, you don't really know him. Well, like I mentioned, I'm his wife, and I just wanted to introduce myself, so you know who I am."

I may not be able to control the actions or thoughts of others, but when they negatively impact me, I will not sit back and accept it. I have the confidence to know I deserve better. Make no mistake, I prefer being respected than liked.

As you continue to grow and evolve who you need to be, you will protect that new energy of self-love and respect you have worked hard to create. You will find that the more you grow to respect yourself, the less tolerant you will be to accept the company of others who do not.

DISCIPLINE

"We are what we repeatedly do. Excellence, then, is not an act but a habit." —Will Durant

Part of self-love is setting goals and higher standards for yourself. And part of self-respect is ensuring that you reach your goals. You must respect yourself enough to know that you are worthy and capable of hitting your goals and getting the results you desire.

Once you believe you are capable, discipline comes into play. Discipline will hold you accountable to reach your goals.

Your discipline guarantees that you follow a set of rules, known or unknown. By having the discipline to live out our values, we can become our true, authentic self, which then has a domino effect for creating the life we desire to live.

Discipline is your ability to recognize that you alone have the authority to determine your choices to get what you need out of your life.

While you may not want to get up an hour earlier, discipline is knowing that if you do not get up, you will not complete your P.M.S. care, the ultimate acts of self-love that set the tone for your day.

Discipline often involves completing tasks that don't offer immediate gratification, but you do them anyway because you desire the long-term benefit. Thus, it requires sacrifice. It is not easy, but you know your hard work will eventually pay off.

It is about commitment. Your efforts must be consistent, and you have to keep developing and progressing. Eventually, your end goal will inevitably be yours.

Do you want straight *A*'s? Then you better take the extra time and effort to study. Do you want to be in great shape with killer abs? Then you better find the time and discipline to put in the extra work. Discipline is skipping out on fast-food when you know it will not help you reach your end goals to be in great shape with killer abs.

When you learn to discipline yourself in smaller aspects of your life, it carries over to larger aspects.

When this habit is developed, you can truly start to see long-term results. Your goals will be accomplished because of the disciplined decisions you made with your habits and routines. With these better decisions, you will start to see areas of your life improve tremendously.

With discipline and accountability, your love and pride within yourself will flourish.

ACCOUNTABILITY

"Stop being a prisoner of your past. Become an architect of your future."—Robin Sharma

I have always been able to hold others accountable for their actions, but I was not so willing to hold my own self accountable for the way my decisions were negatively impacting my life.

To refresh your memory, I was suspended from school; I shoplifted on several occasions. I was arrested, fingerprinted, and charged with a felony for fighting.

Essentially, I had little drive. I never could quite wrap my brain around the fact that all these terrible things just so happened to me. I knew I was a good person, or, at least, it felt like I was; so, I could not understand why it felt like everything bad happened to me. It did not seem fair.

Turns out, all the terrible situations I found myself in were, shockingly, a result of choices I made. My bad choices were a result of flaws in my character. I was not a bad person, but I was definitely flawed.

When your character and values are jeopardized, you tend to make poor decisions. When your values go out the window, chaos will ensue and bad choices and circumstances will be the result. You must change. You must reevaluate yourself. Get connected back to the values that exist deep inside you to guide you and bring back order into your life.

I became a victim of my circumstances that I created. I was quick to blame others for my pain and problems. I felt lost, frustrated, and incredibly angry. I felt like my life was out of my control. Happiness was eluding me.

What I did not realize was that I was only a victim if I did not have control. Yes, things happen to us that we cannot control. In those situations, we can only control our reactions.

But in this situation, which was my life and my future, I was in complete control. I had the power then, just like I have it today and any other day, to change my course of action to impact my future.

So, look at what you do have control over and assume responsibility for it. By doing so, you will begin to build your self-respect. When you have accountability, you can discover your true, authentic self.

Through accountability, you will have an unwavering dedication to your life, vision, and all the values and morals that encompass your character, no matter what.

BE TRUE TO YOU

"Reclaiming your personal power doesn't come from trying to be liked by everyone. It comes from honoring who you are even if others don't like you."—Cheri James

You will never be able to respect yourself if other's opinions matter more to you than your own. I learned a long time ago that not everyone is going to like me, no matter what I do. While I try not to give them a reason to hate me, if living the life I choose is considered offensive to someone else, so be it. If I am true to myself and my values and I am not breaking any laws, then that is their problem, not mine.

What someone thinks about you is none of your business. You cannot make everyone happy, but it is important that you are satisfied with who you must face in the mirror each day. It's best to stay focused on what you can control, which is yourself. We cannot control anyone else's thoughts or opinions.

Do we all want to be loved by someone other than our family? Of course we do; but that will be the organic outcome when we love and respect ourselves.

Please, oh please, do not desperately seek attention or approval. Your worth does not need to be validated by anyone else. Do not give away that authority and responsibility. No one, besides you, gets to determine your worth.

Genuinely be yourself. You will find that the more content and satisfied you are with yourself, the more you will draw the right kind of people.

Let me be clear: I care and respect the opinions of those I love. If someone I am close with tells me I should work on something, I consider it; especially if it seems to be a reoccurring issue causing problems. No one is perfect, and we can all improve to make our lives and those around us better. So, it helps to get feedback from others.

However, whether it is a suggestion for improvement or compliment paid to you, they alone do not validate you. Do not get caught up in the need for positive reassurance about how great you are.

My husband is extremely outgoing and sociable, which is the opposite of me. If I do not know you, I am very shy and quiet. This is often perceived the wrong way. They think I am "stuck up" or "a bitch". I even heard, "She thinks she is better than people." Not at all; but others can make that assumption.

In the past, my husband has urged me to "be nicer" and to "go talk to more people" so people would not think I was a certain way. I have entertained his suggestion, but that is not who I am. If I feel like going to create conversations, I will, but otherwise, I won't.

BE HONEST WITH OTHERS

"Influence is about being genuine." —Johnny Hunt

A part of being true to yourself is being honest with not only yourself, but others. Honesty is the best policy.

I work in one of the toughest, cutthroat environments. It is incredibly competitive, and people lie, cheat, and forsake all of their ethical standards just to possibly make a few extra bucks.

Greed is a monstrous characteristic that sends integrity right out the window for a lot of professionals in my industry. I will never let the opportunity to make more money jeopardize my character.

Don't ever forsake who you are because you feel like it puts you at a disadvantage. It is likely your honesty that is your advantage.

Be genuine; it is the best way to be honest to yourself and those around you. Transparency will grant you respect you didn't even ask for.

CHAPTER APPLICATION

Gaining self-respect is about holding yourself and what is important to you in the highest regard. So, you need to identify your core values and recognize how they impact your decisions and actions. You must uphold your values; otherwise, you are not being true to yourself.

Respecting yourself means loving yourself enough to establish discipline and accountability for yourself.

Once you decide what exactly it is you want, you must do the following:

1) Make a commitment to yourself.
2) Acknowledge the results you seek will not be expedient, but they will provide you with the gratification you seek.
3) Prepare to make sacrifices.
4) Develop a routine and be consistent in your efforts.
5) Stay resilient even with setbacks; remember, every day is a new day.
6) Own your decisions and your actions and do not pass blame.
7) Be responsible with the control you have to make your life better or worse.

It will require distinct boundaries to be established. Conflict is not a bad thing. It can be an opportunity to grow. We just must communicate in a reasonable way that lets others know, *My needs are being compromised, and it is not acceptable.*

Boundaries are the unwritten rules you establish for the relationships in your life. Enforcing them will grant you a greater respect for yourself.

When you are genuinely yourself, you accept your character and are comfortable in your truth. In turn, you will attract the right people. At this point, validation from others is irrelevant. The most important opinion to you needs to always be your own.

6

INNER CIRCLE

"People inspire you, or they drain you, pick them wisely."—Hans F. Hansen

have always been fortunate to have a close circle of friends. It is important to have a strong and loving support system to give you hope and happiness.

We all need emotional support, especially women. We need a shoulder to cry on and a place to vent our frustrations. We need people to have a good laugh with, share our thoughts, and brainstorm ideas.

While we will all lose our footing, and that is okay, we need not be too proud to ask for help. Sometimes we need the help of other people to pick us up, comfort us, and let us know it is all going to be fine when we feel like life is spiraling out of control. Friends can get you through some of your most difficult times.

I may have not had much else in my earlier years, but I always had the best support system within my friends.

I could not have survived my youth and the most challenging obstacles in my life without those beautiful souls. I was not strong enough, so I gained my strength through them.

When I was ten, my parents moved me into a neighborhood that would become my saving grace—not the neighborhood, but the kids in it. The bonds that I formed there were something so special and something I will be forever grateful for.

Those little girls taught me how to be a good friend because they were the best of friends. They always loved me, what felt like, unconditionally.

And I absolutely loved and adored them. They were my family, and we had a strong loyalty to one another. They loved me, guided me, and told me when I was right and wrong, sort of.

They were very smart, funny, kind, adventurous, loving, trusting, and nurturing. They were my comfort and my home. I often was with them because I never wanted to be at my house.

They were there for me when my parents separated, and my mom left. They were there for me through my first heartbreak. They were also there for me when I was bullied and harassed. They were always around through my obstacles and great life lessons.

While I did not have the love I always needed from my parents, I had the love, loyalty, and support from the girls I grew up with. Their support was constant. It grew and only strengthened over time. My difficult situations only brought me closer to them.

My inner circle was my lifeline growing up. Your tough times become a lot more unbearable if you do not have support from at least one other person. If you have just one great friend, then you are blessed more than you know.

Your path will determine what new people you will find yourself blessed with. As my life and circumstances constantly changed, so did my inner circle. Currently, my inner circle includes confident, crazy, funny, and like-minded entrepreneurs.

Throughout your life, new challenges and struggles emerge. Friends will be your sanctuary throughout your journey. Some old, some new, and some at just the right timing. Embrace and value each one of your friends, past and present. Appreciate how fortunate you are to have these wonderful people, as they truly are gifts.

Regardless of your age, your inner circle should be supportive, comforting, and inspiring. Find people whom you have uplifting and positive interactions with; friends who possess characteristics you admire and qualities that you appreciate.

To determine the best people for your inner circle, look for those who have similar values, goals, and aspirations. Here are some qualities I have concluded an inner circle should possess:

- honest, trustworthy, and loyal
- dependable and reliable

- open-minded
- genuine, kind, and caring
- great at listening
- takes initiative to encourage you, challenge you, and believe in you

They should want you to be happy and never attempt to hold you back. Friendship should be mutually beneficial. As I have heard, make sure it is a circle and not a cage.

If certain friendships become more work than they are worth, then it's okay to cut ties. They say you are who you surround yourself with, and their energy influences you. So be careful with your selection. Remember, your energy must be protected at any cost.

Avoid those who are constantly negative and do nothing but drain you. These types of people are called energy vampires. You cannot let those closest to you kill your vibe or impede your progress. When they do, it is time to cut the anchor loose and sail on. No explanations are necessary.

CHAPTER APPLICATION

A strong inner circle gives your audacious mindset the courage and confidence to soar. They are the ones cheering you on to really go for your heart's desire and take the risk. They are also the ones to pick you up when you will inevitably at times fall. No one person should have to travel on their journey alone. They can, but it simply just will not be as easy, enjoyable, or as fun.

Look at who you currently have in your circle. Is there anyone who shouldn't be in your close circle? If so, set boundaries and create more distance.

Do you need more people in your inner circle? If so, get out there and meet more people. Remember, in order to have a good friend, you have to be a good friend.

SECTION 3
CONFIDENCE

"Self-confidence is a superpower. Once you start to believe in yourself, magic starts happening."—Unknown

Many areas of your life require confidence. Whether it is in your career, communications, or relationships, you will need to recognize where you can take action to improve your confidence. It requires intention, and just like other muscles, you must train and build it in order to make and keep it strong.

Confidence comes from a place of self-love and self-worth. When you begin to build on the concepts we covered in the first two sections, you will begin to see your confidence take new heights.

This section is designed to help you recognize the thoughts and ideas that will deplete your confidence and the actions that will help you gain confidence. You must let go of negative thoughts or inactions to focus on the actions that will develop your confidence. Notice how I keep repeating the word action. Your confidence will be decided by the behaviors you choose.

When you are plagued by self-doubt, it becomes much harder to put yourself out there. However, you need to continuously act and accept the idea that things may not work out the way you wanted them to.

You must make a habit of moving past your fear. No one enjoys being rejected, failing, or being uncomfortable by change. However, your response to these types of fears is what will determine your confidence.

Insecurities will breed low confidence. Facing challenges, taking risks, and putting yourself out there will create high confidence. It is much easier to take risks when you are confident in yourself.

If you do not have confidence in yourself, your decisions, and your abilities, you will never be brave enough to take the necessary actions to create an audacious mindset.

7

AVOID NEGATIVE FEELINGS TOWARD YOURSELF AND OTHERS

*"Don't compare your life to others. There is no
comparison between the sun and the moon. They
shine when it's their time."* —Unknown

To stop negative feelings toward others, you need to be secure in who you are. What are your strengths, your superpowers? What makes you special and unique? What talents do you have to set you apart?

I used to struggle with this answer. I did not know. I felt like I was okay at everything but not so great or the best at anything. I was like a jack-of-all-trades—good at a lot of things but really a master of none.

Yet, I have come to learn I can master whatever I really desire. A few of my strengths are my discipline and dedication to accomplishing what I set my mind to.

It is important to become aware of what your strengths and weaknesses are. From there, you can be compassionate toward yourself for things you may think you lack.

Time and experience have developed and revealed new strengths, but at the same time have created weaknesses within me as well. The real trick, when it comes to your perceived strengths and weaknesses, is balancing out the two.

As you look at your strengths and weaknesses, you will notice that your weaknesses are linked to your strengths. You must accept the bad with the good.

You also need to accept that what you perceive as your strengths and weaknesses are exactly that; your perception of them. Your strengths and weaknesses are two sides of the same coin. A strength in one situation is a weakness in another and vice versa.

Confidence comes from knowing your strengths and knowing how to use them for their greatest purpose and benefit. When you know your strengths and accept your weaknesses, you will have an easier time avoiding comparing yourself to others, feelings of jealousy, and judging other's choices.

COMPARISONS

"Comparison is the thief of joy."—Theodore Roosevelt

It's very easy to get caught up in comparing your life and situation to someone else's. With this new era of the Internet and social media, you can easily be convinced that everyone has it all together but you.

Even though we know deep down that this is not the case, we still take the time to compare ourselves with others and feel we come up short.

Regardless if it is a stranger online or someone you know, it is extremely easy to get caught up in comparisons. It is especially easier for our youth and young adults to do this. As Pastor Steve Furtick put it, "The reason we struggle with insecurity is because we compare our behind-the-scenes with everyone else's highlight reel." [3]

When we compare our life to other's highlight reels, negative feelings can emerge like envy, jealousy, resentment, and aggravation. Thus, we only end up hurting ourselves. As we have come to find out, these moments captured on social media are often staged, photoshopped, and filtered so our eyes are deceiving us.

We are all on such a different journey and path that we do ourselves an injustice by assuming our path is not correct just because it is different than someone else's. We damage our own progress when we self-sabotage and think that we are in competition with them, focusing on their path rather than our own.

There will always be someone smarter, prettier, younger, more talented, or flat-out better than you in some area, but they will never be you. Stop focusing on what you do not have, and try concentrating on what you do have.

We all have our own strengths and weaknesses, all of which make us uniquely ourselves. The faster we realize this, the more we can focus on what is best for us. If we are not embracing ourselves, then we are hindering ourselves.

JEALOUSY

> *"Never do the envy, jealousy, and insecure stuff. Be the hustler, the well-wisher, and the go-getter."* —Unknown

At some point, we have all been guilty of being jealous of someone else or something they have. I admit, I have been jealous a few times growing up. Luckily, I never let it consume me to self-destruct.

You must be able to quickly recognize it, so you do not allow yourself to get caught up in it.

This emotion rears its ugly head at an incredibly young age; when we get jealous that our sibling got the last red piece of candy that we really wanted.

Unfortunately, it's one of those qualities that comes naturally. It is a negative quality that can breed despicable behavior and terrible thoughts. It can get grossly out of control if you let it.

When you feel jealous, you often view your opposition as a threat of some type. You justify why they have what they have and rationalize why it is easier for them. Maybe you are jealous because they represent what you want to be or wish you were.

Typically, jealousy stems from seeing a desirable quality that you lack in someone else. Whether it be materialistic, how others feel about them, the energy they give off, or the way they carry themselves; seeing what you want can make you jealous. Jealousy is hate bred from insecurity.

Not surprisingly, it is one of the deadly sins. The way you combat this emotion is with the abundance mentality, which we will discuss more in chapter 21.

I have experienced my fair share of mean girls, bullies, and harassment. It was relentless and exhausting, and it always left me with the confusing question of *why*? I remember people telling me at the time, "They are just jealous." I would think to myself, *No, that can't be. What would they be jealous of? There is nothing to be jealous of.*

Jealousy is the result of those who have low self-esteem. They pass off their feelings, brought on by their own insecurities, on to others. They dislike those who represent what they wish they were or for those that have something that they lack. Jealous people often do not realize that the emotion they are experiencing is, in fact, jealousy.

They despise people for no reason or very trivial reasons. They come up with reasons to justify their disdain of another person. A person didn't necessarily do anything, but a jealous person will find a passion in disliking them.

I have witnessed it on several occasions. Do not let your preconceived notions lead you to think it is only mean girls or petty women; no, I have seen this behavior among a lot of men, as well, as I have gotten older. It may not even be as clear or obvious. It is more of a passive aggressive approach.

If you find yourself feeling this emotion, quickly recognize it, confront it, and release it. When you let go of jealousy, you can begin to focus on what you can do for yourself.

The only way you are going to be able to successfully let go of your jealousy for good goes right back to the first section.

1) Love yourself! Appreciate exactly who you are, your strengths, weaknesses, flaws, and fabulousness. You are enough!

2) Focus on you! Your vision, your goals, your habits, your progress. Journal to see how far you have come along in your journey. Be proud!

3) Appreciate how truly blessed you are! You are improving. Celebrate your success, and the success of others, genuinely. Your time will come.

JUDGMENT

"When you judge another, you do not define them, you define yourself." —Wayne Dyer

Judgment, just like jealousy, is something we all are guilty of. Like jealousy, it is poisonous. Judging can be extremely dangerous because it involves assumptions. We assume both bad and good things and categorize it because it is easier for our brains to process the information.

However, we make assumptions and form opinions so often, too quickly. And when we do that, our perception becomes our reality, but that does not mean it is the truth.

I refrain from making judgments about people and their actions when I do not know them. You never know someone's story and, therefore, you should never judge a book by its cover.

Anytime I may go down that road, I quickly catch myself, a danger warning goes off in my mind, and I get uncomfortable and turn back.

Judgments derive from an individual concluding them and have nothing to do with the person who is being judged.

I have never seen judgment more prevalent than among mothers. Mothers fear that another mom might threaten the way they perceive themselves. Women want to be great mothers because they love their children so much and do not want to feel like others are doing better for their children than they are.

Judgments can be brought upon when insecurities in ourselves surface. A lot of moms believe that they do not have it together compared to a Pinterest mom and are unnecessarily hard on themselves.

Others are guilty of negatively judging how another parent handles discipline, playtime, mealtime, all decisions that are for their individual child, and quite frankly, no one else's business.

Parents like to feel that the examples they are setting, and the values and morals they are instilling, are the best possible. They like to feel validated that they are doing an amazing job raising the next Einstein, president, Tom Brady, or better; at least they would like to think so.

We can easily get caught up in judgment and jealousy, but neither one does anything to help your situation. Do not judge; just remain curious because you do not know the entire situation. When you have the ability to observe without judgment, you learn to rid yourself of negative thoughts and assumptions.

When you start to realize that your focus and energy needs to be on your progress, then you can begin to build up yourself and your confidence. When you love yourself, you will not feel the need to judge others.

TIMING IS EVERYTHING

*"When the time is right, I, the Lord, will
make it happen." —Isaiah 60:22*

Often, when we compare, have jealousy, or judge others, we are just unhappy with what we have or who we are. To fix this, we may want to take charge and just make things happen. However, when we push ourselves too much, too hard, and too fast, we find ourselves being extremely frustrated.

While we do not want to wait for our time and we want to make our time now, sometimes we have to hang tight and let things run their course.

When you are living out someone else's dreams, visions, or expectations, you are not being true to who you are, and it will be hard to determine what your life and purpose should be.

I remember when my best friend and I applied to the same school, hoping we would get in together. It was perfect in our minds; we would be roommates and have so much fun like we always did. Nothing would change, and our adventures would continue.

However, as you can probably guess, that was not the case. She got in, and I did not. In fact, I did not get into any of the three schools I applied to.

I felt alone and embarrassed. I was not that surprised because I told myself she was smarter, she had better grades, and she probably had more credentials. But I was still disappointed.

I put all my eggs in this one basket, and I was left with nothing. She tried to make me feel better by saying, "Just go to a different school and get better grades, then transfer in."

I did not want to do that. I felt very behind as it seemed my whole graduating class was going off to school, pursuing their futures, and I, who could not wait to fulfill my imagined, fantastic life, was stuck at the starting gate.

My only option was to attend a local community college, but I was less than thrilled with that idea. And of course, I eventually failed out. But it did all work out precisely as it was supposed to. There is a saying that goes, "Trust the timing of your life," meaning everything happens when and how it is supposed to for every individual.

We often cannot see it at the time, but when we reflect on it, we realize that a path didn't necessarily end; instead, we were directed on to a new and better one.

If I had gone away like I thought I should have and followed in the footsteps of my friend's dream, I would have lost out on the opportunity to pursue my own path. I would have never met my husband, and it is hard to guess what my life would have been.

CONCLUSION

The time we take to make comparisons is more time away from focusing on ourselves, our improvements, and our progress.

Jealousy and judgment will never allow you to break free out of your mind and pursue action. They keep you worried about everyone else instead of the person who can give you all your heart's desires; YOU. Recognize and capitalize on your strengths. You will inevitably have weaknesses and that is okay, for a weakness likely derived from a strength.

It is hard to be patient and trust the timing of your life, but it is all by grand design and unfolding in exactly the way it is supposed to. You just must believe that. Stay true to yourself and to your course.

8

PERFECTION IS NOT REAL

"Striving for excellence motivates you; striving for perfection is demoralizing." —Harriet Braiker

Let me be upfront and clear; perfection is not real. However, the need for perfection can be. Perfection can be a dangerous irony if you let it get out of control.

Having a perfectionist mindset can be very unhealthy. I know this all too well. I waver on the tedious line of being an overachiever and a perfectionist. My zealous nature can get me into trouble.

I try to balance out my immense drive while accepting my shortcomings because anything taken to the extreme typically causes more harm than good.

Perfectionist traits are self-sabotaging and will diminish any progress and your confidence. You need to work on getting rid of these traits.

UNREALISTIC EXPECTATIONS

It is a great quality to have high standards. However, you need to learn to be forgiving of yourself, others, and situations beyond anyone's control.

You can have high standards, but unrealistic expectations are extreme standards. With unrealistic expectations, you leave no room for error. These expectations are nearly impossible to achieve. They only allow two options, such as black or white, and always or never. In a perfectionist's mindset, you are either a success or a failure.

Unfortunately, when you put this kind of immense pressure on yourself, you minimize any progress you are capable of, and you will be completely defeated by impossible demands.

Review the expectations and forgiveness section in chapter 2.

YOUR WORST CRITIC

When you are overly harsh with yourself, it is easy to feel frustrated and angry. With so many unrealistic expectations and pressure, you will literally self-destruct.

You will become so consumed with fear that it paralyzes you, and you do nothing because you are afraid of doing something wrong or just not doing it well enough. When you fear failure and rejection so much, you become consumed by self-doubt.

Being too hard on yourself will create a downward spiral of other negative actions that will damage any confidence you might have.

You must silence your vicious inner critic demanding perfection. This critic keeps you focused only on the bad and blinded to any good.

If you don't learn how to silence this inner voice, then you will sabotage your own progress and ultimately your goals every, single time. When you allow that critic to get out of control, you will wreak havoc on your inner peace.

PROCRASTINATION

Procrastination will kill any chance of success.

It is perfectly understandable why procrastination is easier and preferred by so many. It stems from the very real feeling of fear.

I remember so often telling myself, if I can just get this script for rebutting rejection perfect, I will go out and make cold calls. I was simply scared to go out and make calls to strangers.

Subconsciously, I was justifying excuses in my mind about why I could not or should not. I would put it off and conveniently run out of time for weeks on end.

I was avoiding this painful act because it would likely lead to rejection and feeling like a fool. However, this was my job. This is a profession I chose, so I knew it was what I signed up for and it was inevitable.

I went back and forth with this tango for years until I finally accepted the truth that things will never be perfect. Neither am I, and that is okay.

Life will never be exactly how you try and plan it out in your mind. For me, a cold sales call made imperfectly is much better than the call I never make but goes perfectly in my mind.

You see, taking action can get you results and move you closer to what you really want, while waiting to do it perfectly will not. Thoughts with no action are essentially useless.

Carolyn Gregoire puts it perfectly in her article, "14 Signs Your Perfectionism Has Gotten Out of Control," that she wrote for the Huffington Post: "The great irony of perfectionism is that while it's characterized by an intense drive to succeed, it can be the very thing that prevents success. Perfectionism is highly correlated with fear of failure (which is generally not the best motivator) and self-defeating behavior, such as excessive procrastination."[4]

Every time we push our boundaries, we discover that the fear was unjustified. The fear we built up so much in our mind pales in comparison with reality. Once we look back, the fear almost seems comical.

Fear holds us down and keeps us captive if we let it. When we conquer our fears, we can move forward without the stress weighing us down any longer.

Overcoming fears will build your confidence. I always remind myself whenever I feel the need to procrastinate, *never put off what I can do today until tomorrow.* Here are some other suggestions that may be helpful as well.

1) Keep things in perspective. It is not that dreadful. Remind yourself of why you have to do it.
2) Do the hardest things first. Get the worst part over as quickly as possible.
3) Set up a time frame in which to complete it or break it down into manageable chunks.

4) Shut down all of your distractions. Your phone, email, etc. You need to stay focused.

5) Stop thinking and just start acting.

6) Know that a reward is coming. Either you can literally bribe yourself with an actual reward, or you can simply feel at ease by eliminating the burden and stress that was haunting you.

DREADING MISTAKES

> *"Never confuse a single defeat with a final defeat."*—F. Scott Fitzgerald

Mistakes, as ugly as they can be, especially for a perfectionist, are necessary. When a perfectionist tries to dodge mistakes, they almost always miss their desired target and goals.

Mistakes are proof that we are trying, and we are growing. Just like no individual is perfect, neither are their actions.

When we avoid mistakes, we are avoiding opportunities; opportunities to gain new perspectives, ideas, and solutions we haven't previously considered.

Our mistakes only stifle us if we let them. We must find the value in what they taught us and then move on. We cannot let them stand in the way of our progress, and we certainly cannot let them compel us to quit. You need to launch into the next action with the same optimism and assurance.

Believe it or not, mistakes are our best shot in discovering our true happiness.

A FAULTY PERCEPTION

"Limits, like fears, are often just an illusion."—Michael Jordan

Overcoming the defeating mindset of a perfectionist has everything to do with acceptance. It is about shifting your perception to line up better with the truth.

A realistic perspective can better equip your mind to see things more clearly when handling the unexpected and uncomfortable. When we are consumed with perfection, we will ultimately get consumed with self-doubt.

When I conduct myself professionally, I want to say all the right things and have the right answers. I want to walk into a new business, meet the owner, impress them, and gain a new client. I do not want to be met with resistance or rejection. However, it happens about 70 percent of the time. And surprisingly, those are decent figures in sales.

No matter how long I prepare, perfect, or procrastinate, those are my odds; seven out of ten businesses that I walk into will reject me. And some will do it nicer than others. But I cannot take their rejections personally.

If I viewed these rejections as personal, my confidence would suffer greatly. I am not saying that some days are not more challenging than others; however, my mindset is that the more I am rejected, the closer I am to having someone partner with me. Those are just the odds, and if I keep playing, eventually, I will win.

This shift in perspective makes all the difference. I must make it a game. The wins are what keep me motivated. The losses must be shrugged off as I'll get them next time. I have no choice but to accept my failures because they are inevitable.

I have trained my mind to love challenges, clearly not because they are easy or comfortable. No, I love challenges because I have proven that I am capable of overcoming them.

My work is a constant demonstration to myself on how I do this. I hurdle over barriers and limitations in my mind. I make what seems impossible, possible, by simply never quitting.

I do not view my actions as mistakes or regrets; instead, I use them as opportunities to learn and experiences to grow from. It is all in my mindset. My confidence comes from knowing, that despite all my flaws, I overcome any obstacle with my determination. I have the moxie to take situations head-on to thrive.

What current perceptions do you have about your own life and career? Do you want to earn more money, advance to a better position, adjust your hours, or work from home one day a week instead of going into the office? Why can't you? Is it because no one else is? Why can't you come up with your own rules and set up different standards? Why haven't you asked yet?

Do you perceive that if you did, others would view your actions as entitled, unappreciative, or annoying? Are you afraid that your boss would tell you NO, and you would feel embarrassed? Even if they did tell you NO, why would it be bad to charismatically keep asking? All you are simply trying to do is advance yourself to a better position in your career.

Would changing careers or switching to a company that could better accommodate you be unthinkable?

Don't ever assume you know the answer. When you master the concept of respecting yourself, speaking up, and having confidence, your abilities come a lot easier. By changing your perception, you can rewrite the rules, push boundaries, and go beyond what you originally thought was possible.

CONCLUSION

You were constructed with all your beautiful flaws and gifts by design so you can excel exactly the way you were intended to.

Honor and accept every single part of you; be gentle and kind to yourself. Mistakes are how we get a better understanding of ourselves. By expanding your outlook, you can better your situation.

If you do not let the idea of perfection go, you will be your own worst enemy for achievement. If you are striving for perfection, you will be too fearful to be audacious.

9

ACT LIKE IT ALREADY

"Courage is the birthplace of confidence."—Debbie Millman

Confidence stems from trust. The exact meaning, according to Lexico, which is powered by Oxford, is, "a feeling of trust in one's abilities, qualities, and judgment."[5] You believe in what you can achieve.

Confidence also means self-acceptance. Again, it starts from within and your mindset. When you are confident, you accept your flaws, feel no need to compare, silence your inner critic, and work with what the good Lord gave you.

Confidence is a choice. It is a skill that takes practice and consistent effort. If you have not yet mastered this concept, then you should at least act like it until you believe it. If you act first, the feeling will follow.

When people perceive that you are confident, you have a great advantage. Self-confidence makes you more respected, more attractive, and more likely to dream and achieve big results.

It is surprising how quickly you will notice situations in your life improving. You become happier as you begin to see optimism, power, and peace within yourself. You are constructing a better you and a better life.

Figure out what areas of your life need attention and more confidence. Start there and even start with minor improvements. You may begin with baby steps, but you will eventually grow to take giant strides.

The tips below are broken down into three different parts. The first two focus on building it within yourself because that is most important, and the last focuses on how to project that newfound confidence outwardly, if at first it does not come naturally.

NOURISH YOUR BODY

We must make sure that we are taking care of our bodies. We only have one body in our lifetime, so if we do not take care of it, it will not take care of us. We need that vehicle to get us to a lot of the places we need to go.

Exercise

Exercising your body crosses the physical barrier into your mind as it nourishes you mentally as well. It is a great way to show yourself that you are accountable and reliable as you prove that you can handle hard work and stay determined. It is a great way to battle your mind when you feel like quitting, to persevere and finish the workout even though your body feels like its going to give up on you. It demonstrates how we can push our limits and do things we did not even think we were capable of.

When you exercise, you are making a commitment to yourself, and when you keep it, you build that tremendous trust within yourself. Physical results are great, but exercise provides a journey and development within your mind that will give you tremendous confidence.

Grooming

Take the time to care for you. Get up, workout, shower, do your makeup (if you wear any), and fix your hair. I do not care if it's only for your dog or your children. Get into the habit and routine of self-care because it is an act of self-love.

Take the initiative to make time to help yourself feel good. Feeling good about yourself does tremendous things to your mood and day. As I mentioned in the first section, if I do not connect all three elements of my physical, mental, and spiritual being to start my day, I struggle. I get through it, of course, but my days are not nearly as wonderful when I do not take the time to "prep" for my day.

Dress

We all love our black stretch pants and yoga pants. Yes, they are comfortable, but they were not designed for everyday wear, or at least they should not be.

I do not care if you are a stay-at-home mom or a student just going to school, mix it up. Use your imagination. Figure out what flatters you and stock up.

I like to represent power and success. My wardrobe represents that I am an important businesswoman, so I love to wear suits with vests, fitted dresses, or pencil skirts with blouses. When I put on this attire, I feel like I can slay any problem or meeting that will happen that day.

Whatever it is for you, get dressed in something that makes you feel great and go out and conquer your day.

STRENGTHEN YOUR MIND

No unworthy thoughts

You must pay close attention to the thoughts you have about yourself. We have already discussed this in chapter 2, but I mention it again here because it is so important. If we do not address these insecurities, we will be quick to beat up ourselves and throw any bit of confidence right out the window.

I think it is important to put it out there and be upfront about what your insecurities are. Set a timer for five minutes to write down any and all insecurities. By writing them down, you can clearly identify what battles you are up against, and you can prepare to win.

When you check back on those in a few months, you will see how your mind has changed and how much progress you are making. You will begin to eventually release those insecurities and let your confidence prevail.

Positive thoughts

Focus on optimism. Any insecurity or self-doubt should be quickly dismissed as you switch gears to your strengths. You must train your mind to focus on all the good you have.

You have to be gentle with yourself. Yes, you may be having a horrible hair day or month, but look how good your mascara looks or how your skin glows. Maybe you did not get that client you really wanted, but look at the great clients you do have and how grateful you are for them. Focus on those things. Eventually, you will do it more naturally.

Gratitude is the key to staying optimistic. It is how you must train your mind. I said it once, and I will say it again; affirmations are wonderful. They take on optimistic ideas with indefinite belief. (More on those in chapter 21.)

Increase your skills

My work is something I take great pride in. I do not want to go through the motions or stagnate and lose my passion. It is easy to lose your passion when you are comfortable or bored. Since I want to be great at what I do, I learn new products in my industry.

I strategize, and I am always looking for ways to refine my craft. I love exploring different techniques or approaches and applying them. I am always looking for a competitive advantage to give me the edge over my competition. I do not settle with the success I have because I know I am capable of more.

My inner circle either must look at me like I am crazy or with admiration. I am always trying to better myself. Whether it be with a new exercise program, writing this book, or going back to school to get an interior design degree, I am always pushing my boundaries to be the best version of myself.

I want to discover my truth and see all I am capable of. I like to prove to myself repeatedly that I can be trusted to achieve anything I put my mind to.

You are improving yourself when you learn new things. When you think you know everything, you really know nothing. Continuous learning is a great way to build your confidence.

So, figure out an area of weakness, and decide how you can strengthen it. And look at what skills you need to build on your path to success. You can find online classes, YouTube tutorials, trade magazines, articles, blogs, etc. There are so many avenues for continual learning. As Ben Franklin said, "An investment in knowledge pays the best interest." [6]

PROJECT YOUR PURPOSE THROUGH BODY LANGUAGE

Confident body language typically comes into play after you have mastered internal confidence. When you can feel good about yourself, you naturally project your confidence through your body language; not always, but typically.

Yet sometimes we can train our bodies to behave confidently, even if we are not completely secure and comfortable acting in certain ways. This is the whole fake-it-till-you-make-it concept.

A career in business has taught me how to pay attention to what my body language is telling others about me. I have had to fake it on several occasions because if I am not confident in my abilities, then why would a prospective client feel confident in choosing me? Why would they trust someone who clearly does not trust themselves?

You are painting a picture whether you know it or not. Here are a few things I am very conscious of, and you should be, too, if you want to project confidence.

Smile

Smile genuinely. When you do, you appear friendly and approachable. It is contagious, and that makes others want to smile back, just like a yawn. It is strange how a smile can lift your spirits and those around you. It spreads kindness. It makes others want to comply with your requests. Most importantly, it creates joy for you internally, so do it more.

Posture

Keep your shoulders back in a straight line with your head held high. It is good for appearing confident, but it is also good for your body and proper alignment. It is never a good look to be hunched over; it looks cowardly. I must remind myself, especially when sitting, to lean back. I will notice my posture is suffering because my back is aching a little. The right posture should send the message that you are relaxed, self-assured, and poised. You are secure.

Gestures

It is essential to have a secure grip and firm handshake. That aggressive shake lets others know you are confident and ready to talk. A good handshake demonstrates a leader with enthusiasm.

Be wary of any gestures that make you appear nervous. Uncross your arms so you appear open, don't fidget with anything, and maintain a relaxed composure. I often think of the image of a duck. Cool and relaxed on the surface and a racing maniac underneath.

Eye contact

I am naturally shy and introverted, so eye contact with random people makes me uncomfortable. However, from time to time, I do like to push myself to make eye contact with a random person in a store or during special events.

There is nothing quite as gratifying as commanding a room. I walk in and make eye contact with whoever looks my way. Try challenging yourself to do the same.

Speak up and speak clearly

Do not silence your needs; claim them. Get what you want by simply asking. She who does not ask does not receive. Do so assertively, clearly, and immediately. Pause if you need to gather your thoughts, but make sure you state them. Do not mumble, and do not stutter. What you have to say is important, and others should listen.

CONFIDENCE EQUALS SUCCESS AND HIGHER EARNINGS

As you work on yourself and implement the above suggestions, your confidence will grow. Remember, confidence is determined by the behaviors you choose.

It has been debated whether monetary success is attributed to higher confidence. I can tell you from experience, higher earners have higher confidence. I'm sure their confidence has only grown as a result of successful experiences, but the initial belief in themselves is what has allowed them to pursue acts that the average will not.

According to an article posted on CFNC.Org, "Self-Confidence: A Key to Success," "People with lots of confidence in their capabilities approach difficult tasks as challenges to be mastered rather than threats to be avoided."[7]

When you are confident, you are more motivated, you set bigger goals, and you push yourself beyond your comfort and past your fears. You are more likely to act, rebound better from losses, and demonstrate optimism, knowing you are in full control.

You value yourself, know your worth, and are not afraid to ask for just compensation.

Confident individuals are authentic and true to themselves as well as their values. They value their time, and they do not discount their abilities. Understanding what you can bring to the table will ensure that you will never settle for less than you deserve. Confident individuals demand more.

Confidence seems to come much more naturally for men than it does for women. The earning gap between men and women should be a clear indication that more confidence among women is required. The only way women are going to be able to shrink this gap is by improving the way they value their worth.

Confident, capable people are highly sought-after, and they should be. Therefore, they have and will continue to be among the top earners. Simply increasing your confidence will increase your income.

CONCLUSION

As I mentioned in the beginning, confidence affects all your relationships. It determines your personal growth just as much as your professional growth. More confident individuals achieve more overall success than those who lack it.

The love and respect you give to yourself will be emulated by others. Confidence will not just make you feel better within, it will also create the changes to improve your overall life. It empowers you in such a way to take charge and control of yourself and your situations.

10

PRACTICE

"Practice creates confidence. Confidence empowers you."—Simone Biles

No matter what type of training you are going through, it's likely not anything that will come easily or automatically. You must put in the time, energy, sweat, and effort. Otherwise, you are not going to get the desired results. Consistent repetition creates confidence.

This is true any time you are striving toward your goals. Practice and prepare with a sense of purpose.

To do well in my career, I created scripts that I thought sounded impressive, and I would go over and over them to get myself a meeting. I memorized them so I knew exactly what to say. I also practiced and prepared thoroughly for rebuttals and objections. Then, of course, I had to put that plan into motion to get the work.

In general, I have more confidence knowing that I prepared, and I am ready to take on what is about to happen. Planning for potential outcomes can make you feel in control even with uncertain possibilities.

Confidence is just like sales, a numbers game. The more action, the increased likeliness of encouraging results. Repeating confident acts ensures your chances of achieving confidence. The more you practice it, the better you get. From there, you adjust, improve, and your confident rituals become habits.

Practice the habits below to build not only your confidence, but to also improve your character, relationships, and life.

LISTEN

When you learn to listen, you can discover a lot, especially who people are and how they like to be treated. When you show a genuine concern for another, you quickly discover what is important to them.

Listening goes along with empathy. Listening helps you build deeper and stronger relationships. When you are focused on another person's message, you will become a better negotiator and persuader, if you so desire. So be quiet, interested, and unassuming.

A reason I have success in my job is that I am a good listener. Most people assume you must be a charismatic fast-talker, but you cannot provide anything to anyone if you do not know what they want to begin with. You cannot assume their wants.

It is particularly important to realize that you cannot learn anything if you think you know everything. You do not know everything. Sit back and observe. It will be much more beneficial and serve you better in the long run.

Confident people can be silent because they do not need to prove anything to anyone. They are comfortable with themselves. When people feel like they are truly being heard by you, your confidence and communication skills will soar.

LAUGH

Always keep and strengthen your sense of humor. Do not take life, or yourself, too seriously. Otherwise, you may end up disappointed. Life has a funny way of keeping us grounded. No matter how much we try and prepare ourselves and hold ourselves to certain expectations, life is unpredictable. Really, the unpredictability is what makes life beautiful and wonderful.

I find humor in my job a lot because, so often, it can be incredibly stressful. It can be hectic and frustrating dealing with technology and things that you cannot control. I must take that negative energy that is building and release that emotion in healthy ways.

When someone is having a reoccurring issue with one of my devices, and they say they have tried everything, and I can hear the aggravation in their voice, I calmly ask, "Have you tried throwing it out the window yet?" We both chuckle and laugh at our ability to recognize that it is a frustrating situation for both of us.

I assure them we will get a solution. I obviously recognize who I am dealing with when I apply humor to situations. I can cut through the tension with a little bit of humor, so the negative feelings do not build and become overwhelming to us both.

Sometimes you just have to revel in chaos, smile, and laugh it off because what else can you do? If you can add happiness in the way of humor to someone else's life, you should. So, practice implementing humor in tense situations and see what it can do for you and others involved.

HAVE PATIENCE

Patience is not one of my strong suits. I know I am not alone either. Everyone wants immediate gratification. To feel like we are making progress, we like to see results immediately. We want to know that our hard work is paying off, and we are moving closer to our desires.

You must remember, it is more about the journey than it is about the destination. Patience goes along with trusting the timing of your life. You must stay the course. You have got to be consistent and persistent with your own actions. As Joyce Meyer said, "Patience is not simply the ability to wait but the ability to keep a good attitude while waiting."[8]

Being patient is a type of wisdom that grants confidence. You have to hope, trust in your abilities, and be patient while receiving the outcomes you desire.

CONTROL YOUR EMOTIONS

My dad had a great saying that I live by. It can be applied to so many facets of your life: "Never let your emotions insult your intelligence." When you can master control over your mind, you will have the ability to control your emotions.

When you are confident and secure, it is much easier to control your emotions. Maintaining a sense of calm and steadiness will allow you to observe a situation more clearly. As Prasad Mahes said, "The mind is like water. When it's turbulent, it's difficult to see. When it is calm, everything becomes clear." [9]

You have to be patient to assess a situation without getting consumed by your emotions. Sometimes your heart can fool you and make you act irrationally. By not allowing our emotions to run wild and unchecked, we can see things logically.

Logical thinking is ideal when dealing with others in your personal and professional relationships. When one is confident, you don't need to be loud or irrational in communication.

You can practice controlling your emotions by, once again, listening to gain empathy for another and their position. Be patient with your response. If you can, walk away and stay silent until you can calmly address the situation. Understand that their position does not diminish your own. They may feel one way and you another, and that's fine.

Treat others with the respect you would want to be treated with. Losing control of your emotions will not help you to find logical solutions. The ability to create logical solutions will increase your problem-solving skills and build your confidence.

GET COMFORTABLE WITH BEING UNCOMFORTABLE

Logical thinking can be beneficial when it comes to your relationships with others; however, it is not necessarily beneficial for decisions you make for yourself.

Logical thinking can deter you from taking risks. You can easily talk yourself out of just about anything with enough reasoning, justified or not. "Don't kill the magical and mystical with logic; they exist in two different spaces." [10]

Being uncomfortable is where growth and learning occur. This is where our boundaries are expanded, and we begin to push ourselves. We discover our capabilities. This is such an important element when it comes to building your confidence.

Practicing being uncomfortable is what will take you to new heights. You should start small. Pick an area in your life that you want to develop your confidence in.

Maybe it's socially. Try once, every day for two weeks, to start up small conversations with strangers. It could be your waiter or the clerk who is cashing you out.

If that is still too scary, then start with eye contact and a smile. You will be so surprised how these little things you incorporate into your life can have big impacts.

If you continue to keep trying new things, you will keep building on your new confidence. Time after time, and example after example, will show you how capable you are of achievement, even in ways you would not have previously imagined.

These new achievements will elevate your confidence. Again, it is all about progress.

BE KIND

It is so simple, yet its impact can be enormous. It may be easily forgotten or dismissed, but small acts of kindness can have significant effects, both on others and ourselves.

Since everyone has their own struggles and we never know the journey the other is on, it is so important to be kind and respectful of one another. Having empathy and understanding for another is not always easy, but it is necessary. Words can live in another's head even long after we forgot we spoke them.

Be positive, be encouraging, and be genuinely kind to everyone you meet, for the kindness and joy you bring to others can influence you more positively than it does for the receiver.

It directly impacts your mental health and well-being. Kindness upholds your integrity. When you live your life with integrity, you are being true to yourself, and trusting yourself is what confidence is all about.

BE ADVENTUROUS

Sometimes you must pick up and leave, traveling to new places, trying new things, and meeting new people.

A great memory from my youth was when I traveled across the US after my mom had left, visiting thirty-eight states total. It was the best experience I had ever had. We stopped everywhere to take in beautiful parks, monuments, and attractions that highlight everything our country is. We stayed in campgrounds all along the way.

I recommend it to anyone. It makes you feel so alive yet so small. This adventure was one that gave me a new perspective and granted me a new hope when I felt so much was lost.

Do whatever you need to do to give yourself permission to experience something different—whether you decide to ride a bike, hike in the woods, take an art class, or whitewater raft. It can be big or small. Allow yourself to break out of your daily routine and comfort to do something new.

New adventures can often allow us to see things in a new way. You gain better insight when you see the world in new surroundings.

New adventures will excite you while also building on your character and confidence.

CONCLUSION

Practice is where focus and intention come into play. Consistency is essential. Self-confidence is about preparation. You must plan, prepare, and practice with purpose.

If you are repeating confident acts, you assume the role of becoming more confident. By taking the time to practice the suggestions above, you will not only become a more confident person, but you will also build skills to become a better person.

SECTION 4
WARRIOR

"You're a diamond, dear, they can't break you."—*Unknown*

I feel like I have been fighting my whole life to overcome odds and expectations while being at a disadvantage.

Perhaps feeling like I'm at a disadvantage is what gives me my edge. I may always continue to think this way because it is part of who I am. My strength heightens when my back is up against the wall. In that moment, I will fight through self-doubt and insecurities to reach my potential. I will fight for my tranquility and freedom.

Warriors never give up. They may get knocked down, but they will not stay there because they are tough. They keep going. They are so focused, committed, and passionate about their purpose that no obstacle can stand in their way.

Warriors are the ones who have recognized that they are in control, and they have the power to make a difference, so they are consistent in their efforts and are resilient enough to never stop until they reach their desired outcome.

Think of the well-known people who overcame obstacles and failures to triumph in success and even change the world. I want to discuss a few to remind you that everyone has their own struggles they deal with.

Michael Jordan was cut from his high school basketball team. Vera Wang's fashion empire was founded on her failure at Olympic figure skating.

Did you know Dr. Seuss had his first book rejected by twenty-seven different publishers? Did you know that Babe Ruth struck out more times than he hit home runs? Walt Disney was told he "lacked imagination and had no good ideas." He founded a studio that went bankrupt.

There are several examples of people that are quite famous that got to where they needed to be because of their resilience and fighting nature.

Perhaps my favorite stories are those of Thomas Edison, Colonel Sanders, and Lucille Ball. Thomas Edison and Colonel Sanders failed over a thousand different times. Sanders was fired from over a dozen jobs over his life and didn't even achieve success until he was completely broke at age sixty-two with only a social security check for income.

Thomas Edison was thought to be too stupid to learn. He failed over 9,000 times to get an electric light bulb to work. But according to Edison, "I have not failed. I've just found 10,000 ways that won't work." He has 1,093 patents in his name.

Lucille Ball was not your typical female in her era. She wasn't at home tending to the house. She was aggressively pursuing her career. She had many films fail, or at best, were average. She went on to create her own magic with her own show and, eventually, her own production company. No one even wanted to pick up the pilot of the beloved, and one of my favorite shows, *I Love Lucy*.

I will give you just one more, very recent example, and that is our 45th president, Donald J. Trump. He staged, in my opinion, the biggest political upset of all time. I do not care if you like him or not; that is not the point. This man is a fighter.

Not one poll, political expert, or pundit got it right. I remember watching the news, just a few weeks before the 2016 election, that convinced me there was absolutely no way for Trump to get to 270 electoral votes.

Yet, President Trump persisted by attending rallies and staying consistent with his message. His dedication, his instincts, his confidence, his tenacity, and grit kept him going all the way to 1600 Pennsylvania Avenue.

I love these stories because of the fighting human spirit these individuals represent. They embody that of an audacious mindset. They fight for what they believe in. They are confident and know what they are capable of. They take risks, and they never give up until their vision becomes reality.

11

POWER

*"I survived because the fire inside me burned brighter
than the fire around me."*—Joshua Graham

SELF-ACTUALIZATION

*"There is nothing outside of yourself that can ever
enable you to get better, stronger, richer, quicker, or
smarter. Everything is within. Everything exists. Seek
nothing outside of yourself."*—Miyamoto Musashi

It is important to point out, that whether you believe it or not, the only power you need to change your circumstances is within you. The only person responsible for saving you is yourself. You create the path you must walk on.

It may be overused, but that is because it is the most relevant lesson when it comes to recognizing your power, which is the belief in yourself. In *The Wizard of OZ*, Glinda, the good witch, said, "You've always had the power, my dear. You just had to learn it for yourself." She went on to explain that she could not just tell Dorothy that because Dorothy would not have believed it. Dorothy had to realize and discover it on her own.

I loved that movie as a child. I watched it constantly. There are many lessons in that beloved classic that helped Dorothy along her journey and will help you, too.

- Have courage and compassion.
- Be a great friend.
- Every one of us is unique with our own struggles.
- Dream big and push past your boundaries. "Dreams that you dare to dream really do come true. If happy little bluebirds fly beyond the rainbow, why oh why can't I?"[11]
- Confidence is what will help you to pursue your dreams.
- Stay persistent on your path.
- Sometimes the simple and obvious solutions are right in front of you, if only you had a better perspective.

To access the power within you, just like Dorothy, you will need to realize the power within yourself and realize your strengths and weaknesses, so you can change or transform to reach your desires.

Self-actualization is about understanding your limits and capitalizing on your unique skills, talents, and knowledge. This concept can mean different things to different individuals, but it is a progression.

We evolve, and so do our continuous improvements to make us the best version of ourselves. The process of reaching our full potential provides contentment.

For me, self-actualization is about acceptance, appreciation, clarity, compassion, comfort with the unknown, a calmness, confidence, and peace.

DETERMINATION AND WILLPOWER

"There is no force more powerful than a woman determined to rise."—Unknown

Once you hit a point of self-actualization and realize you have the power within, you need to use your determination and willpower to make the changes you see necessary.

Willpower will help you stay in control and make smart and necessary decisions. Determination is the relentless intention to ensure your goal is achieved. While I look at determination as the destination, willpower is the journey to get you to that destination.

There will be roadblocks, challenges, and limitations that will test your commitment. Will you use your stumbling blocks as stepping-stones? How about using your failures as lessons learned to make your next approach a little wiser? Or will you give up because the challenges are too hard?

Determination seemed to always come naturally to me. When I really wanted something, I would do everything in my power to get it. I see remarkably similar qualities in my daughter, as she does not take *NO* for an answer. It is truly exhausting as a parent, but I laugh thinking how much I admire that quality.

I remember looking through *Victoria's Secret* magazines as a teenager, mesmerized by these gorgeous women in great clothing, especially the business attire. Ingrained in my mind was an independent, polished woman in a suit jacket with a matching pencil skirt, high heels, and a briefcase, crossing the street of a busy city.

I was intrigued by the image of success she represented. She looked in charge. I did not know what her job was, but I knew that when I grew up, I wanted to be her.

I had no idea how far I would eventually take myself to craft that childhood fantasy into reality. I set my aims high on financial independence. I obtained it more than I thought was ever even possible.

I quit my job and started from the bottom in a career I knew nothing about. It was strictly based on commission, so I was going to make what I was worth.

That is an uncomfortable thought when you make nothing at first. You are guaranteed nothing. All your hard work feels like it is done in vain because you aren't seeing any of the results of your hard work initially. I was rejected, uncomfortable, and questioned my choice for taking on this new challenge a lot at first.

At times, your willpower will waver. This is when your habits and rituals we discussed in chapter 4 will guide you back on track.

I had no office to report to and no accountability in how I chose to spend my time. I had all the freedom to do what I wanted. However, every chance I got, I was studying, preparing, and practicing to be great at my new role.

I never stopped knocking on doors or putting in the time to guarantee success. I had thrown myself overboard into the ocean, and I had tremendous determination and willpower to keep swimming instead of sinking.

I never stopped. My goals increased every year, and I was hitting them while working part time and as a brand-new mother. I had weathered the storm. I was not merely proceeding, I was exceeding.

I set a goal so scary for myself that I thought it was unlikely, but I did it with high hopes. Sure enough, in the following year, I achieved it.

I reached a pinnacle in my career and became a part of the six-figure earnings club. It was magical and quite unbelievable.

How was it that a girl from the wrong side of the tracks, living in a small town of West Virginia, where the median annual income is $38,000 according to DQYDJ.com, with limited opportunity, achieve that success?[12]

The answer is quite simple; it is because I was no longer that girl. I had the determination and willpower to change. Like a phoenix that rose from the ashes, I remade myself.

I may not be the supermodel on those pages, but I have accomplished that important, independent role that I aspired to be so long ago. I was aspiring to achieve much more than merely my earnings.

Looking back, I realize that what I was in search of was something far greater than money. It was not about earning more, but it was about becoming more. I desired to have my own identity, autonomy, and freedom.

I was in control. I wanted to change, and I was going to make it happen. I claimed my power. This was a turning point in my life where I discovered to never doubt the power within because you can reach whatever you desire.

The very same could be said for you.

If you are focused, you will find a way; if you are distracted, you will find an excuse. Realize that change is possible, and make the commitment to yourself and see it through. Determination and willpower are habits, so you can decide to cultivate these new habits which are necessary for change.

CHANGE

*"The lust for comfort kills the passions
of the soul."*—Kahlil Gibran

Before change can even be accepted, you have to have a strong enough desire, want, or passion. Once it is determined that your desire is strong enough, the next step is change. This is a scary word for so many, as it requires challenging your comfort and exploring the fear of the unknown.

If your life isn't where or what you want it to be, then change is necessary. You must determine what area of your life is not giving you the happiness and harmony you deserve.

It may require you to remove people from your life that aren't good for your soul; it may require a career change to pursue your real passion; or it may also be to lose 20 lbs. to jump-start a healthier lifestyle.

Often, we make excuses to avoid changing. For example, many who want to lose weight use excuses, such as, "I don't have enough time, I don't want to pay for a gym membership, I don't like going to a gym, I'm too out of shape, I have bad knees, I work all the time." Or, "I can't eat healthily because it takes too long to food prep. My spouse picks up the groceries, so I eat what's available. I can't plan out my food for the week because I don't know what I'm going to want to eat or have time to make. My kids have so many after-school activities. We are always on the go." And the list goes on and on.

In reality, they just don't want to change. Living healthy is hard, and it does require work, as does any type of change. But not changing is also hard. For example, gaining weight is hard, feeling tired all the time is difficult; feeling bad, insecure, and depressed about yourself is also terrible. The difference is that the hard work required for healthy living is justified way more with the results you genuinely want than the alternative.

As Jim Rohn said, "We must all suffer one of two things: The pain of discipline or the pain of regret and disappointment."[13]

Whatever change you want to make, it will begin with recognizing within yourself that change is necessary.

CONCLUSION

When you discover a burning desire within you, you will change to take flight and discover new heights in the effort of reaching it.

You will become so committed and focused on your desire, no obstacle or barrier will deter you. It is not as much about the destination that you seek. It is more about the moments, lessons, and discovery within yourself.

"There is wonderful freedom and joy in coming to recognize that the fun is in the becoming."[14]

When you find out what you can do and who you can become, that is the most gratifying reward. Reflection is important because it will allow you to clearly see your transformation and admire how far you have come. The best way to reflect on your progress is through journaling.

So, is it creating who you need to be in order to fulfill your vision or is it the discovery of your potential that has been deep within all along? You decide!

Regardless, what transpires is a magnificent evolution.

12

PERSISTENCE

*"A river cuts through a rock not because of its power,
but because of its persistence."*—Jim Watkins

Persistence is a term I have heard several times throughout my career. It always seems to come from prospective clients who either are annoyed or impressed with my ability to keep showing back up, even when they have already told me no or that they are not interested.

While most people go away, never to be seen or heard from again, I make a habit to politely follow up to see if circumstances have changed. Because, as it turns out, situations are always developing, worsening, or changing.

Success can be the result of those that do the same things repeatedly, combined with altering circumstances. For example, when I call on prospective clients, they may tell me no again and again, but maybe one time when I walk in, their circumstances have changed and they say yes.

Other successes can be the result of persistent actions that each time differ in a more developed, experienced approach with the knowledge gained from previous failed attempts.

Persistence says a lot about your character. It shows that you are a hard worker, that you are focused and determined. It is a demonstration of how badly you really want it. Quitting is not an option, and nothing will stop you from reaching the outcome you want.

My persistence guides me daily in my career. You see, I have no boss; I have no colleagues to impress; I have no accountability or responsibility to anyone but myself.

Do not get me wrong, it can absolutely be great. However, if you don't have the motivation or discipline and can't seem to find it within, staying persistent is very challenging.

I cannot tell you how many days I had where I was turned away repeatedly. I didn't want to make one last call and torture myself any further, but I did. I did it, and it ended up being the golden egg that I almost missed finding.

At times, I have thought, *No, I probably should not waste my time calling on a prospect,* and it ends up being a great client. My persistence to keep trying led me to great clients. It was also my continued persistence throughout my career that has guaranteed my success.

When I was about seven or eight months into my career, I was approached by a gentleman who told me he knew I had been trying to call on his clients, and it was just a waste of my time. He offered not-so-friendly "words of advice," and warned me against pursuing his clients.

He told me that most don't last a year in our industry, and I probably wouldn't either.

My confrontation with him actually motivated me and made me more persistent. I was already experiencing some success, but he confirmed it to me that day that I was doing all the right things. Otherwise, he would have never been so compelled to confront me.

He was scared, and he was worried. I was a very real threat to his success, and that is why he wanted to deter me. I was not going to let him bully me, nor intimidate me, and I certainly was not going to back down; nope, I had a new motivation to try harder.

I like being told I cannot do something because it only makes me want to prove the naysayers wrong. Maybe it is because I am a fighter, and I am not afraid of conflict.

I'm going to be honest, if I ran into him a few months earlier, he may have persuaded me negatively because I faced all the struggles he mentioned, but I knew I had finally just started making progress, and I believe he was sent as a reminder to keep going. I was on the right track.

Too often, you give up right before you are on the brink of something great. You get deterred by roadblocks, hurdles, and every type of adversity imaginable. All these things, I feel, are by design to test your commitment on how badly you want something. Keep pursuit! You are so much closer to a breakthrough than you even know.

13

RESILIENCE

*"Life chips away at us all. Some play the victim.
Some choose to be a survivor. And then there are
those who choose to conquer."—Unknown*

When my dad told me my mom left a note saying she was not coming home, I was in total shock and disbelief. I didn't understand, and my eleven-year-old self couldn't wrap my brain around the fact that my mom really wasn't going to come back. I had so many questions. *Why?*

The note simply said, "I'm done you can have her."

My dad was angry and very open about what she had done. I remember trying to call her over and over again many times, but she would not answer. One time, I pleaded with her to come back. I was yelling and angry. She told me, "This is why I left. You are the problem. It's your fault. You're a brat."

I wondered if this is what happens when you are a bad kid; your parent leaves you.

The few times I did see my mom, she would often recount the horrible abuse my dad inflicted on her. I was angry at him, but it seemed she was trying to make herself look better by pointing and blaming him. My dad would do the same thing, pointing out all of my mom's flaws.

I was so lost and so very alone. You think growing up, you know your parents. I didn't know either of these people. I lost so much trust and felt completely abandoned. I told myself from that day forward I had only me, myself, and I to depend on. I was only eleven, and I had to find a way to get by until I was eighteen so I could try and leave everything behind.

As time went by, things got easier. I healed; the pain lessened. You, too, will heal, and the pain you experience will lessen as you adapt and adjust to your new normalcy.

When they say kids are resilient, they are not exaggerating. Resilience starts with acceptance. You have to be able to adjust and embrace change. You must learn to adapt in order to keep moving forward with hope for better.

You must let go of the anger, the resentment, the sadness, and all of the negative emotions brought on from hardships because you are wiser and better because of them.

What invaluable lessons can you take away from your own hardships?

When you start to recognize what you have gained from your experiences, it is a lot harder to be bitter about what you lost.

My life took a dramatic turn at a young age. I was forced to grow up way too quickly and figure out how to adapt and survive. It shaped me in a way that is both great and not so good.

I could easily blame my fucked-up childhood for a lot of things that didn't go right for me, but that would only allow me to grant power to something other than myself. I made a lot of mistakes, and I learned enough wisdom through valuable lessons that some people are never even granted in their lifetime.

I feel so blessed and grateful that, although I am damaged, it has strengthened me.

CONCLUSION

The damaged can be the most dangerous because they know they are resilient enough to survive anything—just as long as they don't self-destruct in the process.

You do not have to shut out your darkness; just don't let it consume you. Honor your darkness, but also be willing to show your light, which is your endurance and fortitude. Be proud of what you have overcome, not ashamed.

SECTION 5

PASSION

"Never settle in this life. Remain open to the possibility of magic and chase the things that ignite your soul's passions. We were born to live, not simply to exist, and within you is passion enough to set this world ablaze."—Becca Lee

More than an emotion or a temporary feeling, passion is strong; it is a burning desire deep within you, so compelling that it summons your deepest aspirations and values that are vital to you.

Passions stimulate and fulfill you. Finding your passion can be a long journey. When you don't have a passion, it will be hard to stay motivated, persistent, resilient, or enthusiastic about what you are doing.

A lot of people go through life never being true to their passions and deepest desires. When you do not discover what your passions are, it is much harder to discover what makes you truly feel alive. So many people go through life, just simply going through the motions, instead of having the passion to make their life exactly as they want it.

There is something so joyous about discovering what ways we can contribute to the world with our unique gifts and skills. Finding your passion will help you to find your authentic self.

When you live your life pursuing a passion, it is much easier to be compelled to take decisive action. Passion drives motivation. A strong enough passion will wake you up in the morning and get you out of bed with enthusiasm because of what you know you are going to accomplish in each day.

You will be highly motivated to get what you want. Your strong desire will allow you to find a way to make things happen. A passionate want will create a way.

When you figure out what you are passionate about, you naturally excite yourself and feel enthused. Enthusiasm is the energy and aura you surround yourself in. They say to become enthusiastic, all you must do is act enthusiastic.

Just as when you smile you feel happier, when you act enthusiastic you feel electrified and that energy is contagious.

You want that enthusiasm because it will help you reject your fear. It gives yourself and others an optimistic energy that we all crave. It is an attractive quality that will make others want to be around you and do business with you. With an enthusiastic approach, you can easily increase your happiness and even your earnings.

APPRECIATE YOUR CRAZY

"No great mind has ever existed without a touch of madness."—Aristotle

I am a little crazy. But I feel like a little craziness is necessary to pursue your passion.

I have always admired those with a little craziness because it means they are authentic and blunt. They are the ones brave enough to be themselves.

To be audacious, you are going to have to channel that inner crazy and pursue your heart's desire. Give in to your passion.

My career requires me to tap into my crazy, adventuress side.

Something is exhilarating about not knowing the outcome. I do not know what is going to happen from one day to the next, but that's what drives me. It is what makes me feel alive inside. How boring is it to go and do the same thing, day in and out, like the movie *Groundhog Day*?

I have good days and bad. Brave days, and days I want to hide in my office. Some days, I get things so built up in my mind that frighten me, and then I face them. I get out of my head and just act. I get so uncomfortable with the thoughts of the uncomfortable unknown, the risk seems worth my sanity.

Unfortunately, many get so comfortable in the status quo that they fear progress and forgo excitement. Progress is hard; it requires work. It means learning, growing, and making sacrifices; but without it, we cannot truly be content.

As I have gotten older, I am much more reserved. Only those who know me well know my crazier side. It is hard to reveal that silly side as a "grown-up," and a "professional" who needs to be taken "seriously."

However, it is important to not push that part of yourself away long enough that you start to lose sight of her. That part of you contains your magic. I think it is important that we never really lose that inner kid. The lighthearted, fun, fearless, spontaneous goofball. The one who believes in happy endings and that anything is possible. They have got something magical we can learn from and apply.

"Do not stop thinking of life as an adventure. You have no security unless you live bravely, excitingly, imaginatively."[15]

CONCLUSION

To have an audacious mindset, you really must master the mentality of not worrying how others may perceive you. You must be crazy enough to take risks and indifferent enough to not get caught up in your performance or the audience's critiques.

You cannot let anyone else's thoughts or opinions sway you one way or another. If you care and worry too much, it may, in fact, be what holds your crazy back from taking the risk in the first place.

When we push our limits, we surprise ourselves by doing things we did not even know we were capable of.

15

USING ANGER FOR GOOD

*"Anger, like a fire, is a primal force. When left unchecked,
it can be destructive, yet when managed and used
wisely, it can be a beneficial and powerful instrument
that leads to enlightenment."* —Moshe Ratson

Anger can be considered a weakness of mine. It is a weakness derived from a strength which is my passion. I am deeply passionate about many things, such as my life, my relationships, my family, and my career.

While my anger has improved over the years, it has gotten me into trouble. But remember, there cannot be a shadow without light. So even though anger has quite the negative connotation, and believe me, I know why, anger can have some positive qualities.

I am by no means advocating for anger and encouraging rage monsters. I have spent time in therapy dealing with this very real, aggressive, and perhaps destructive emotion.

Today I can contain my anger, but I cannot make it, or the things that trigger it, disappear, and I have accepted that. The silver lining is that we all can control the appropriate level of this tricky emotion to produce constructive and favorable outcomes.

DEBILITATING ANGER

Whether it's genetic or it was brought on by my circumstances, I have had this emotion for as long as I can remember. I also held on to it for quite some time. It negatively affected my relationships. It got to the point where it was severe enough to harm my most important relationship; my relationship with my husband.

After the birth of our children, I would lash out at him often. I am not sure if it was the hormones, the dramatic change, loss of control, the list could go on, but regardless, it was unnecessary and unhealthy. I would lash out and justify it in my mind that it was his fault. He was making me angry. I would think, *If he would only do things a certain way, I wouldn't get so mad.*

That was my irrational thinking. It was so deep and so very real, but I didn't even understand why or where it was coming from. It was vicious.

After some much-needed reflection on my past, it was hard to avoid some underlying issues. My behavior had to change, as I was totally trapped and consumed by anger. To do this, I had to let go of things and allow forgiveness. The only healthy way to deal with it was to let it go. I had to release the anger I held towards my mother. I know, this is much easier said than done. However, you must allow forgiveness of the pain and hurt in the past in order to have a healthier future. You are not forgiving a person because they necessarily deserve it; you are forgiving them because you deserve it.

Anger is toxic if you hold on to it and consume it. A great book that helped me a lot was the *Anger Trap*. It puts a lot in perspective.

When your anger is interfering with your most valued relationships with those closest to you, then it's time to change. It's that old saying from Buddha, "Holding on to anger is like drinking poison and expecting the other person to die." It is never worth it. That negative energy is damaging and can destroy your soul.

MOTIVATING

These days, my anger is a lot more helpful than hurtful. In work situations, I use my anger to help motivate me.

To be successful, I have to obtain new clients and retain my current clients. Competition interferes with my success, resulting in frustrating situations that anger me. Because I know success is ultimately what I desire,

I have to stay sharp and focused on what I need to accomplish. I use my anger to drive me to success because it motivates me to do the following:

1) Stand up for myself by protecting my values.
2) Shift my focus on what I can control.
3) Find better solutions with pure determination.
4) Fulfill my goals.
5) Gain positive insight to figure out what I can do better in order to improve myself and my circumstances.

Anger is not simple, and it can be quite complicated. Therefore, constructive anger requires patience, critical thinking, and often, self-reflection to move to resolutions.

As one of my great mentors, whom I never met, Jeb Blount, points out in his book, *Fanatical Prospecting*, "Anger is just energy, and when you harness that energy, you tap into a powerful force. In fact, one of the enduring qualities of highly successful people is the ability to turn disappointment, defeat, and anger into unmovable determination. When someone hurts you, your body and mind fill with energy and adrenaline for revenge. Take advantage of that gift of energy to get better because achievement is the ultimate revenge."[16]

Recently, I found myself in a situation at work where I felt angry and very betrayed by a man I had a good working relationship with. We partnered together with complimentary services, and we shared a good bit of business.

My industry constantly changes, so, of course, he ended up paired with a direct competitor of mine.

He brought me into his office to discuss how we were going to deal with our existing clients. He asked me why I "even bothered doing this thing," aka my career. "It's piddly stuff."

He was referencing the fact that I did not really need to work. I took his comments to mean I needed to step aside and not get in the way of letting him do his job. He said, "Your husband makes enough money."

Once again, I felt a sense of pride because he clearly viewed me as a threat. At the same time, I was mad at his approach. I calmly sat across from him, and I let him know that I had every intention of pursuing his clients.

We already knew that before I even showed up to his office that day, but, once again, it was an intimidation tactic where it was assumed I would back down and fold. I knew that he was my fiercest competition and that the battle would be difficult with hard losses, but it only motivated me to charge forward.

My anger about that whole situation drove me to new heights, in a good way. The fact that he devalued my career, treated me lesser, and acted as if I was not as deserving as him infuriated me. I was more ambitious and determined to achieve success than ever before. I continue to work harder and protect my interests with everything I have.

CONCLUSION

Debilitating anger is simply your brain being lazy. Motivating anger is when your brain is activated. This type of anger drives your brain to intensely focus on your desired end result. However, be careful your anger doesn't slip into debilitating and allow yourself to get caught up in things that don't advance you to your desire. Don't let your emotions insult your intelligence.

Motivating anger forces you to learn, improve, and adjust yourself and your circumstances until you reach your end goal. Debilitating anger that lashes out with no constructive effort will only make you and your situation worse.

You must find a way to use your anger, or any of your perceived weaknesses, to work in your favor.

16

LOVE

WHAT LOVE IS NOT

"Women, you are not rehabilitation centers. It's not your job to fix him, change him, parent or raise him. You want a partner not a project."—Julia Roberts

Every young person has someone that comes along who makes them feel so special and experience something they have never felt before. This happened to me when I was fifteen years old.

While the boy was quiet and did not have many friends, he piqued my interest. He was so handsome, and I wanted to know more about him. We eventually started talking more and more on the phone, and that brought me such happiness. Everything was rainbows and butterflies. I had such a giddiness every time I was in his presence. I was in love. This lasted for about ten months.

After that time, he started pulling away. He was no longer returning my calls. He would get irritated and angry with me for no reason. I did not know what I did wrong, but I knew something was not right. Sure enough, my intuition screaming on the inside was correct.

My friend had told me that he was cheating on me. Of course he was cheating with a girl I never really cared for to begin with, and now she was the interest of the boy I had fallen so hard for, the boy I was in love with.

I had so many questions. I did not understand. How did this happen? Why did he want her now and not me? Was she prettier or better than me? She must be; otherwise, why would he choose her?

I was mad, heartbroken, crazy, jealous, bitter, and I felt defeated. Every range of emotions I enjoyed so much the previous month was sent crashing down like a wave of despair.

I cried over and over and over again, pleading with him to change his mind. I was so sick on the inside, I could hardly eat.

Honestly, I did the most pathetic things I've ever done in my life. I found out he was at the movies, so I decided to lipstick his car while he was inside, spitting and writing obscenities all over it.

It was immature and crazy. It was the prelude to the video of Carrie Underwood's "Before He Cheats." I am not sure what I was hoping to accomplish by those actions. I guess I wanted him to be mad and angry just like I was.

I will not be too hard on myself because I was young and in unfamiliar territory. I was experiencing, learning, and failing. I not only lost this new love, but I lost all self-love and respect.

I remember him telling me that our situation was my fault, that I was to blame for his cheating. All the questions continued. I thought, *Maybe it was my actions. Maybe I did do something to provoke this.*

Eventually, reality set in for me. It was time to start thinking with my head and not my heart which is so difficult when you are in love and blinded by the heart.

Of course, it wasn't my fault. So, let me be the first to tell you, this is the biggest lie you will ever hear from a cheater or a mistreater. No, it is not your fault. It is always the fault of the cheater and the mistreater. It was their decisions, choices, and their actions all along that caused the destruction.

It was so odd because even though I knew that I deserved better, I was still hoping he would come back. I tried to play hard to get by talking to other guys, which worked in getting his attention, but I was tired of playing games. I finally just had to hear it. I asked him if he ever loved me. He was hesitant the first few times I asked until, finally, I heard the words I dreaded but somehow found closure with; I do not love you.

It was a crossroad in my life, and I appreciate him for telling me those words still to this day. Maybe he never loved me, or maybe he did but not enough; either way, it did not matter. I knew there was no going back. In my mind, I had lost. The door had closed, and our story had ended.

It is easy as an outsider looking in to see the obvious. Actions speak louder than words. I did not need him to tell me it was over; he clearly checked out long before I did. However, it was difficult to accept that it was time to let go and move on. I suppose it's our ego that makes us cling to things that have already dissolved.

It was hard to feel the abandonment, the self-pity, the questions, and the agony again. But it was real, and it was there.

That heartache shook me to my core. From that moment on, my walls shot up like cannons. I vowed I would never allow myself to feel that vulnerable again. From that point on, I played the game of collecting hearts while concealing my own.

The funny part was, I loved the passion I got within myself experiencing love but, looking back, I hated who I was or who I became during that roller coaster. I was needy, dependent, and most importantly, I lacked self-respect. I put his needs above my own (which they say that is what love is); however, the problem with that is, they were not being reciprocated.

I was weak and pathetic and willing to settle for less than I deserved. I became that, and that is not why he was initially attracted to me. How could I expect love from someone else when I was not loving or being true to myself?

Love is not giving your all to someone who doesn't give back. Love is not tolerating being mistreated or holding on because you believe you can change that person. Love for another also doesn't require you to sacrifice your self-love or independence. Love is not dishonesty, uncertainty, or disrespect. It should bring out the best in you, not the worst. Love is not pain but can be when you love the wrong person.

Listen to your intuition. Chances are, if you have to constantly second-guess your relationship, you are in the wrong one.

WHAT LOVE IS

"A soulmate is the one person whose love is powerful enough to motivate you to meet your soul, to do the emotional work of self-discovery, of awakening."—Kenny Loggins

The most magical love is the kind you never see coming. It finds you. It strikes you almost like lightning. That was my husband. He made me believe in love at first sight. It was magical, unanticipated, and passionate. He was so beautiful and charismatic. It was so easy to fall so hard as he easily crumbled the walls I had spent years building. Though I tried to compose and shield myself, I was no match.

Our love story is not only my favorite but, of course, in my opinion, the greatest. Probably because it never should have happened. Fate, timing, and a force stronger than both of us pulled us together like two magnets. It reminds me of the Chinese proverb of the invisible thread.

They say things that come so quickly leave just as quickly. All I can tell you is that our souls connected in a way that will stand the test of time. Here we are, seventeen years later, and I still find myself falling for him. He is, and always will be, my one and only.

We faced numerous obstacles throughout our relationship, but we never wavered. We will likely continue to experience new challenges as we both evolve. However, we are both fighters who are passionate in what we want, and that is one another.

Love is never easy all the time. Love can be complicated, but love should never be too difficult and too hard. It may not always be easy, but it shouldn't be a battle to make it work.

Everyone deserves a love that is unshakable, strong, positive, and uplifting. The kind of love where you are with someone who is your better half. Someone who sees the potential in you that you don't yet see in yourself. Someone who brings out the best in you.

If you want to improve and grow together, then you need someone who motivates and inspires you and is your biggest supporter and encourager. If this doesn't ring true for you and your partner, then I suggest you re-evaluate your situation. You have options to fix it together or let it go and find the kind of love you deserve.

Love is the most beautiful gift you can find. But to keep this gift, you must work at it. To keep love, you need to be dedicated and committed, just like with everything else. It will require work, and it should never be one-sided. You must remember that love is a verb, meaning it requires action. Thus, you should demonstrate acts of love daily.

It requires open communication, especially when life is quick to get in the way and demand other priorities. You must make time for one another because at the end of the day, that is your partner, your best friend, your soul mate.

No one can make me laugh quite like the man I am with. He makes things easy. He is quick to keep things in perspective. Life is too short to get caught up in things that are not that important in the grand scheme of life. He reminds me of that always, especially in my most stressful days.

Our love brings me such incredible joy. The kind I have never known before. Time has only secured and strengthened our bond. We are a team.

While the love I have for my soul mate is so peaceful and comforting, it's also adventurous and free. That is what makes it so beautiful. It is a constant adventure because we evolve and change together. My heart is at peace because it is free.

CONCLUSION

A lesson in love is an invaluable experience. It may take several experiences to know exactly what you do and do not want from a partner; what is acceptable and what is not.

Until you learn to love yourself enough, no one will be able to love you in the way you need to be loved. I'm not suggesting that you have to love all parts of you or be a master at self-love, but what I am saying is that you must first know that you are worthy and capable of love. You must know that you are not worth any less just because you may not yet see your own worth.

Once that happens, you can find true love; the love you never see coming. You cannot force love. It grows organically, or at least it should.

Love is much more than just falling head over heels for someone. There is no doubt that the passion must be there, but it is more. It is about being with someone who motivates you to do better in life.

Your partner should be capable of bringing out the best in you. They should inspire you to become the best version of yourself every day, as you should for them as well.

So, don't settle for less.

SECTION 6
COURAGE, NOT FEAR

"Courage is not the absence of fear; it is the conquest of it."—William Danforth

While we cannot control many things, we can control our thoughts, behaviors, and actions. As I write this book, the coronavirus has taken a massive hold on our world. Our lives, economy, decisions, and everyday life have dramatically changed. Many gave in to fear and panicked, stockpiling supplies.

It was a challenging time. Yet through any hard time, we can have the courage to confidently plow ahead because we control our thoughts. We do not have to give in to the fear.

While we can, and should, do everything we are able to, sometimes there is already a determined outcome by a higher power and there is no fighting that.

For me, I fear what I do have control over, which is crazy yet comforting. I fear things that are a result of my mistakes and actions.

I fear being a bad mom, having a marriage that could fail, not having a successful career, embarrassing myself, or saying stupid things that cost me a client. My biggest fear is failure, but I am in control of that, also, to ensure it does not happen. That helps to put my mind at ease.

When you apply courage and face your fears, you will often find that what frightened you was mostly imagined. As FDR stated, "There is nothing to fear but fear itself."[17] Our minds absolutely play tricks.

A reaction of our mind is designed to perceive dangerous threats with real purpose for our survival. This survival mechanism is known as the fight-or-flight response. It is an instinctual, physiological, rapid response to danger.

Stressful situations send off an alarm in your mind, which in turn activates the hormones in your body to appropriately respond to a perceived threat. It is primal and happens very naturally and automatically.

Unfortunately, what helped our ancient ancestors recognize harmful situations, nowadays, it is often misguided and seizes our abilities to pursue risks.

Having courage is about acknowledging the fear but still proceeding forward with action. You take risks regardless of the fear and doubt. You must be fully focused on your intentions. Be prepared for obstacles and adversity, but do not hesitate to confront your challenges. Hesitation will only hold you back from getting what you really want.

17

AUDACITY

"Fortune favors the audacious."—Desiderius Erasmus

I remember getting my first job with my marketing and business management degree. I was an advertising account executive at a radio station, which was just a glorified sales job. I had to train and go into businesses in the territory assigned to me.

Because I had a great manager and team, I learned a lot. It was exciting as it felt like my first important job where I had a nice title, independence, and responsibility.

It was challenging, like every new job can be, especially when it comes to sales and figuring out if you can cut it.

While I was not very successful, I still had a decent enough base salary to help me not feel as though I was completely lacking.

After a few months, I found out I was pregnant. I was bound and determined that even after I had my baby, I would be back to work.

Everyone at the office told me that I was probably not coming back, but I knew better. I had just started my career, and having a child was not going to change that. I wanted to be a successful career woman. Being a mom was not going to be all that I was.

I never even wanted to be a mother. I never really thought about it, and I could not imagine it. Motherhood was not a priority for me.

After I had my baby, everything changed. I get choked up thinking about the fact that I almost allowed myself to miss out on the most miraculous experience.

As they tell you, an instantaneous love forms after giving birth. A bond that is so strong is molded and unbreakable. To be a part of such a beautiful, unbelievable, incredible experience puts your life in a completely different perspective. It is as if time stand stills and nothing else matters other than that beautiful baby.

Words can do it no justice. Only experiencing it will put it into context.

I knew that I had changed, and I would never be the same. I would not do things for my own interest but in the best interest of my daughter. I would do things that would make her proud. I would be the female role model that she would aspire to be, someone she could look up to. I wanted her to have the absolute best, and I felt like the only way to give her that was to be the best I could possibly be for her.

Thus, I knew I could never return to my job. I would never leave her to go work for someone else and fulfill their dreams. I had to fulfill my own dream.

Luckily, my husband has a unique gift to recognize opportunity. I remember when we first moved back to West Virginia, he suggested I should take on an industry that had not been tapped yet in our area.

I always thought, *No way. I could never do that. I do not want to do that. How would I do that? There is simply no way.* I was completely frightened by the idea of failure. I did not know how to sell; I did not have any product knowledge; and no local companies were around to train me.

It was such a crazy notion to even propose. I just did not think I was capable, and I did not believe in myself enough to take on such a risky idea. So, I conveniently came up with all of the reasons why I shouldn't and couldn't. I put it off for five years.

All those excuses and reasoning went out the window when I would hold my baby and think long and hard that I had to figure out something for her. The doubts were still there, but I was laser-focused.

My only option was to dive headfirst and do it. I knew it was the time to take that leap of faith. I would have to figure out the details, but I was going to do it, and the how would have to follow.

Failure would not be an option for me because I would not allow myself to quit. I knew that setbacks would all be part of it, but this was something I had to do for my daughter.

There is no motivation quite like your children. When you take action for something that is far greater than you, you have more purpose and meaning behind it. I was so frightened yet so excited for this new adventure.

I remember studying and studying like I was in school. It is an extremely complicated industry that is relentlessly changing. I was intimidated, but I was also confident that I would be able to be successful. I knew I could be taught anything.

After about six months, I was breaking even, and what I made went straight to daycare. While that might seem frustrating for most, I knew I was close to breaking through.

I was set in motion, and there was no stopping me. It sounds laughable, but I had a warrior mentality.

I had my terrible days that left me questioning whether it was even worth leaving my daughter for. I remember being in my car pumping milk in between appointments.

Sometimes, I would be driving down the interstate with my cover around my neck to ensure that I was pumping every three hours. I had to make sure I was drinking plenty of water and eating enough to ensure I had an adequate milk supply, because when I wouldn't do that, I'd get poor results and I would get frustrated. I remember stopping even at the gas station rest areas to rinse out all of my pump Medela parts. I had a cooler that I would always have to travel with to store the milk.

This was time-consuming and took away time and energy from my work, but breastfeeding was also a commitment that I was not going to sacrifice.

There were many challenges, struggles, and stresses that would make me wonder if what I was doing was even worth it, but in my heart, I knew it would be. I was working part time and making progress.

As a parent, you go through this incredible guilt. Someone else is raising your child. You are missing out on little things because they grow so fast and change at such a rapid rate.

What new first experience will you forgo if you are not there? Will your bond be as close? Am I selfish for leaving to pursue my career?

All of these things go through your head, but I also knew myself enough to know that if I didn't do what my heart was calling me to do, I would always be left with the question of *what if. What was I missing out on? Who am I? What am I capable of?* I know that being a mom may be my greatest accomplishment, but my identity is not defined as my daughter's mother.

I could not sit at home with her and wonder if this was all that I was meant to do or be. I was convinced that I could have it all. I could find that middle ground where I would take on the amazing role of a mother, but also fulfill my dream as a successful businesswoman.

In this scenario, it did not have to be all or nothing. It was the first time I realized that I could have it all, and I intended to do so. I would have my cake and eat it too. I was the boss of my career and my life, so I would make the rules.

People often mention the great quest for balance. They like to say it is impossible, but I like to defy the odds. It can be hard, and you will struggle, but you can obtain it.

I am not saying it is easy, but an alignment within yourself, priorities, and tradeoffs, you can achieve a balance you desire. It is a tricky tightrope to walk, but you know what priorities need your attention the most at different times.

I can always make more money, and if I feel the need to, I will, but it will never come at the expense of an invitation to one of my children's events.

You can achieve the perfect balance and determine your happiness. You just need the audacity to know you can create it.

To be audacious, you must be daring. You will not be able to take bold risks if you don't believe in yourself and your passion. Audacity demonstrates that, regardless of the outcome, you trust yourself enough to handle whatever may come your way.

CONCLUSION

You must be true to yourself. You cannot let your dreams or your life slip by. When you begin to start making progress toward your desires, you will always be met with challenges that tempt you to settle for comfort. Do not do that. Revel in the chaos, and step it up a notch.

I initially thought motherhood would be my Achilles' heel; as it turns out, it was through motherhood that I discovered a new passion, a new strength, a new motivation, and my limitless potential.

TAKE ACTION

"You may never know what results come of your actions, but if you do nothing, there will be no results."—Ghandi

To overcome fear and embrace your courage, you need to take decisive action. Decisive action is deciding, without too much contemplation or worry, about whether it is the best choice. Sometimes you need to rely on your heart a little more and your mind a little less, and as a result, you will become fearless.

Much success is obtained when you are pushed to do things before you are ready. You must tackle things head-on, improvise, and evolve.

We cannot just sit there and think and dream all day long. We must have the courage to take action. Beautiful ideas are just that, ideas.

I had the idea to write this book long before I actually did so. I prayed earnestly to find out if it was what I should do. But even after knowing and receiving signs that I should do it, I let self-doubt creep in. However, eventually, I just took action and started writing.

You can easily combat self-doubt by simply acting.

Acting will help you play offense instead of defense. Make moves. Take initiative before it is even necessary. You must be proactive and play to win. Do not play the game not to lose.

Get out of your comfort zone because if you do not, you're not taking the risks necessary in order to win and win big. Playing it safe will keep you comfortable but will result in lost opportunities.

BE BOLD

"She was never quite ready. But she was brave. And the universe listens to brave."—Rebecca Ray

When Beau and I were dating, he told me he was going to move to Michigan for work and asked me to come with him. I was not exactly thrilled about the location, which did not really seem like much of an improvement over Pittsburgh, but I was always up for an adventure.

My only hesitation was that I was making so much progress with school and had just two semesters under my belt. I disliked the idea of basically starting all over. I chalked it up as a trade-off and knew it was what I wanted to do. I would find a way to work out everything else.

Several times, friends, co-workers, and customers asked if I was crazy. People would tell me all their opinions about why it would not work out.

It made no sense to them why I would leave behind everything for a man I did not know that well. I just thought, *If the relationship doesn't work out, it's really simple; I just move back and pick up where I left off.* Nothing lost, nothing gained.

However, the move was not just for a man. This decision was also about me and a new opportunity. You are only young once. I had a new outlook and path I was on. You have to be willing to take bold risks and not take advice from someone who is not where you want to be. You won't get where you want to go in life without being bold.

So many would rather stay in their comfort zone than push beyond their limits to find out what's behind a new door. I can tell you that every time I have been brave enough to leave the good, I always find something better. It is so true that, sometimes, when you risk nothing, you risk everything.

DARE TO DEMAND

Every event in your life is an initiation teaching you how to take your power back."—Unknown

Often, on our journey, we are tested or tempted in good ways and bad. I was familiar with overcoming obstacles and challenges. I was not familiar with the temptation of low-hanging fruit, even though it was appealing, because it appeared as an opportunity.

A beloved veteran at a larger, local bank was interested in having me fill his position when he retired. He worked with some of my clients, and I already knew a lot of his clients because they were very loyal to him and politely and reluctantly rejected me. However, I never stopped asking, and we ran into each other on several occasions.

We respected each other and developed a pleasant bond over the years. He was already twice retired but loved what he did. He was very much ready to retire for good, and he was adamant that he wanted his position filled by me. I was very much flattered at the thought of filling his important position with a significant role.

I was approached by the president and vice president to interview for the job. I was so nervous. I really wanted that job because I would have been making an extra $15,000 annually than I was currently making, not to mention an extra $60,000 in potential bonuses every year. I would have a fancy title, recognition, and a layup of leads and businesses already handed to me. It sounded so cushy and like a perfect opportunity. I was excited.

However, my husband told me not to do it. I thought he was insane, and I was irritated at him because I didn't understand why he wouldn't want me to take this position. His reasoning was, "If you do take the position, that bank will own you."

Scary thought for someone like myself who values independence, freedom, and lives life by my own set of rules. He said, "You can easily make that money in the next few years if you keep doing what you are doing." I went on the interview, and we agreed if they would bump up their base offer an extra $10,000 and only require me to work four days a week, I would accept the position.

I cannot tell you how uncomfortable I felt asking for more because I undervalued my worth. They did not accept my conditions, and I did not get the job.

However, it was a great thing. My earnings easily doubled their offering in just a few short years, and I got to dictate my schedule and only work part time.

At first, I was obviously disappointed. I mean, they basically concluded I was not worth it. Shortly thereafter though, it became abundantly clear that what I thought I wanted would have come at a far greater cost.

I now know how much I am worth, and to think, I almost settled on discounting myself. I was so afraid that if I did not accept that position, I would miss out on earnings, a great position, and recognition. Instead, I had to let go of the good for my great to come.

That door closed, and a better one opened. I earn more than I ever could have with them. More importantly, I kept my freedom and what I truly value; a higher recognition and respect within myself.

HESITATION ONLY HINDERS YOU

> *"If you are unsure of a course of action, do not attempt it. Your doubts and hesitations will infect your execution. Timidity is dangerous: Better to enter with boldness. Any mistakes you commit through audacity are easily corrected with more audacity. Everyone admires the bold; no one honors the timid."*—Robert Greene

In order to take action, you need to learn to not hesitate. There are far too many people living with regret—whether it was their choices, actions, or decisions they made or did not make. Some go through their life wondering how things could have been.

Those that take positive action with a good outcome often regret not acting sooner because they find the original fear that held them back had no justification. Fear will cause you to hesitate and misjudge a situation that warrants action.

Hesitation, while mostly the product of fear, has other contributing factors as well. People who hesitate often lack confidence in themselves. They don't know how to trust and believe in themselves or their decisions. They doubt their abilities and settle with the choice of doing nothing rather than making a decision that could be wrong. If you find yourself hesitating, you are being indecisive; and being indecisive is a result of overanalyzing.

Indecisive individuals may have too many opinions and outside views clouding their judgment. Others just may lack experience in making decisions because decisions have mostly been made for them.

Through my experiences, I have learned a few lessons to prevent hesitation:

1) Get a hold of your fears by confronting them; otherwise, you give your fears power to grow bigger, stronger, and bolder. If you run and avoid conflict for too long, you only make things worse.

2) Make a bold decision. Do not try to go around, climb over, and avoid the obstacle; instead, break through it. When you proceed forward, even when scared, you take back your power, self-respect, and peace of mind.

3) Stop wasting your time. Decide and move on so you don't have to contemplate *what-ifs*.

How can you overcome hesitation?

1) Start becoming assertive. Practice making decisions. While you may need a little confidence in order to make a decision, the act of making decisions will contribute to your confidence as well. Your decisions can be as simple as the outfit you're going to wear, the restaurant you are going to eat at, or your plans for the weekend. No matter how insignificant it seems, it does matter, so make a choice. The better you get at making simple decisions swiftly, the easier more difficult decisions will be.

2) Confront the consequences. Lay out a list of pros and cons if the decision warrants it. Knowing the potential outcomes makes it easier to decide what direction and decision you need to take. Sometimes, what you thought was a mountain in your mind was actually just a molehill you can deal with.

3) Employ KISS. Keep It Simple Stupid. You don't have to overcomplicate and overwhelm yourself or a situation. See things clearly

for what they are, not what you think they will be. Don't worry about a mistake with a bad decision. No matter what decision you make, it can always be corrected with another decision.

When you do these things, you take back your control and assume power for your decisions, actions, and life.

CONCLUSION

Fear can become a habit, and a terrible one at that. Do you know what I have found to be the only remedy for fear? Action. Action cures fear. Action will require you to make moves before you are ready. Any decision I make, whether it be big or small, that I feel fearful about, I revisit my past situations where I have trusted myself and proceeded forward full speed. The outcomes have always seemed to be in my favor, and I know I must act.

To perfect your ability to overcome your fears so they do not hold you captive, try doing something you fear every, single day. Of course, make sure to take baby steps.

Have you ever really examined the things you are afraid of? Try writing them down, examining them, understanding them. Shine a light on those fears deep within yourself to see how much warrant they deserve.

Whether it's confronting a bully, asking for a promotion so you don't get passed up, starting a business, developing a healthier lifestyle, or leaving an unhealthy relationship, the faster you make an effort to improve your circumstance, the better off you will be.

You stop being the victim and start being a victor simply by taking initiative. Time is of the essence. Do whatever it is you need to do and do not hesitate, for that will only hinder you.

19

FEAR, THE PHONY

"Doubt kills more dreams than failure ever will."—Suzy Kassem

IMPOSTER SYNDROME

Every so often, I question my abilities. When I find myself doing that, I must remind myself that it was not luck. It was the result of hard work and dedication. Every accomplishment I have was not by accident.

When you start falling prey to self-doubt, you are experiencing a real event known as the imposter syndrome, where you feel like a fake or a fraud. You doubt what you have already proven yourself capable of and don't give yourself any credit.

It is a term that I heard a few years back, but a feeling I could strongly relate to. I think the more you have struggled with self-love or insecurities, the more often you will be plagued with this doubt or fear within yourself.

This concept revealed itself frequently in my career and pursuit of financial success. I suppose it is because financial independence was always my biggest insecurity. I always feared I would never achieve monetary success and that I would fail in achievement.

These days, I try not to let my fears trick me, but this struggle continued within me for quite some time. I would notice this imposter syndrome or feeling of inadequacy was present a lot throughout my career.

It was odd because even though I was doing great, I felt like it was not good enough. I felt that, at any moment, it would be taken from me or all fall apart because I was not good enough to handle it all. But, of course, I had proven that I could.

When imposter syndrome creeps in, reflect on your past successes. You do not have to fear failure. Doubt your doubts before you doubt your abilities.

FEARING THE JUDGMENT OF OTHERS

I remember back when I started making good money and wanting a nice vehicle. While I was proud that I earned the right to drive around in whatever vehicle I wanted, I worried how it would come off to potential clients.

I felt embarrassed driving my SUV, feeling like I would be judged negatively for pulling up in a vehicle that was expensive. I worried that it would appear that I was full of myself, or that I only could afford a nice vehicle because I was overcharging clients. Completely ridiculous, but I would have these thoughts.

Now it is of no concern to me simply because my mind has shifted. Even if someone comments, "Wow, that's a really nice vehicle," I simply reply, "Thanks," with a smile. The fact is, I can afford it because I'm really good at what I do, so I don't need to feel ashamed of that.

This goes back to cultivating a strong self-love and sense of self-worth. Even after you have cultivated that, you will have moments where you fear the opinions of others; but just remember, you are stronger and better than that. You do not need validation from others. Have the courage to own your own view of yourself.

CONCLUSION

If you find yourself falling prey to your insecurities, shut them down quickly, and remind yourself that those claims are baseless.

To combat this, it helps if you keep a success journal or a success jar. That way, when imposter syndrome creeps in, you can go back and reflect on your successes.

It is so important that you silence the sound of that inner voice that criticizes you because it is not being truthful. Your truth is whatever you desire. Do not live with past failures, self-doubt, or self-limiting beliefs. You have learned how to overcome your past, and you are capable of great things.

SECTION 7

FAITH

*"Always pray to have eyes that see the best in people, a
heart that forgives the worst, a mind that forgets the bad,
and a soul that never loses faith in God."*—Unknown

My life is very quick, exciting, and thrilling, a complete adrenaline
rush. It is wonderful and amazing. I am so grateful for it. I really
could not ask for much more. Yet, not too long ago, I felt empty in
a sense.

Everything I worked so hard to achieve, I had. I was financially independent. I had a successful career, great friends, the best husband, and the
most beautiful children; so why wasn't I satisfied?

I felt guilty, ashamed, and ungrateful for feeling like this. I kept making and achieving new goals, pushing myself further, and learning more;
yet, somehow, I was incomplete. Something was missing. How could I
have a life so unbelievably blessed, yet I wasn't fulfilled?

I am sure you figured it out, quite simply, based on the name of this
section; but it was the result of an absence of divinity, a higher being or
higher purpose. For me, that is God. Others call it the universe, the al-
mighty, source energy, the holy spirit, or their inner guide. Regardless of
what you call this higher power, it is part of your spiritual being. It is very
much a part of who you are, so you must connect with it.

I had a very inconsistent relationship throughout my life with my spiritual side. As a child, I felt very spiritually connected. In my youth, I spent
many nights in deep thoughts and wishes under the stars and talking to

123

the moon. I would ponder ideas with heightened curiosity. As I got a little older, I lost that side of me.

I never went to church and knew nothing about anything written in the Bible. The few times I did interact with churchgoers, I got a big dose of the Bible-pushing judgers who basically said going to hell was inevitable unless I was a saint. Unfortunately, while their intentions I'm sure were good, and they were passionate in their cause, I didn't like how they communicated their message, and I wasn't going to be scared into submission.

From that point, I was a self-proclaimed atheist, but I don't even believe that was the way I really felt. My dad talked about his religion of Eckankar, and the most I knew about that was the concept of karma, which had an appeal to me.

Throughout my late teens, twenties, and early thirties, I had minimal connection with my spiritual side. I felt awkward. I did not know what to say, how much to say, what was right, appropriate, or even how to connect. Yet, since nothing else seem to be fulfilling this desire within me, I was bound and determined to give it a try.

The first time you do anything, it is always a bit awkward until you practice. Like with everything I have done in my life, I chose to learn; I just kept doing it until it became more comfortable. I went to church. I read. I started meditating. To help me meditate, I found an app on my phone to help guide me through the process.

I received a book in church, known as *40 Days of Prayer,* to help those looking for a better journey. This book showed me how and even gave me suggestions on what to pray for. I did not do everything in the book, as I wanted to start small. I would make it more of a priority to see what happened. I flirted with making time for it until finally, it was apparent that my best days started with prayer, appreciation, and scripture.

I have now been consistently including it in my morning rituals every day for a couple of years. I cannot tell you the serenity and satisfaction I have found within myself.

You can only take yourself so far without connecting on a level much deeper than your own presence. I have read enough books and educated myself enough to know that belief in only what you can see will limit your journey. You must have faith in the unknown and the unseen. It is your spirituality that will guide and fulfill you as your faith connects dots and allows you to be your true and authentic self.

My faith has helped me when I felt lost, lost my passion, struggled with anxiety, obstacles, adversity, or simply the unknown. It guides me and directs me because it taps into my inner compass. It helps me to be fulfilled, happy, and at peace. It provides a comfort and calmness that gets me through my most challenging times.

My life has experienced incredible highs since embracing my faith, spiritual being, and a higher purpose. It is almost mystical how things just keep getting better. The best part is that I am aware now to recognize my life unfolding in such a beautiful way. I am not simply going through the motions. I am living my life the way I was intended to.

When you know you are capable of more, I strongly suggest connecting with your spiritual side to discover what exactly it is.

20

BELIEVE

*"When the roots are deep, there is no reason
to fear the wind."— African Proverb*

Believing is powerful in itself, for through it, we craft our reality. Our thoughts, ideas, and actions are shaped by what we believe. Therefore, the belief in yourself and of something greater is tranquil and magical. Throughout the book, I have discussed ways to believe in yourself:

1) Believing you hold a power within to positively change your life.
2) Believing that your hard work and practice will get you to your visions and goals you know are possible.
3) Believing that change is inevitable, and that you yourself have to change to fulfill your passion and purpose.
4) Believing you possess an inner strength, reminding you that you are strong enough to handle anything, regardless of your circumstances.
5) Believing you can make an incredible impact on those around you. Things you say and do matter, no matter how small.

While you must continue to believe in yourself, the belief in something higher will be your guide, your comfort, and your strength all along the way. You see, believing in a higher power creates awareness, more positive thoughts and emotions, and a more fulfilling life with purpose. We seek to have a more meaningful connection because we are spiritual beings.

The wonderful part is that there is no one right way, religion, faith, practice, idea, technique, or way to connect. You can meditate, go to church, pray, read inspirational literature or scriptures, or just simply sit in silence with your thoughts. Just experiment to figure out what works for you.

I do not claim any specific religion, practice, or belief; but I do find truth or recognition and respect for them all. I have heard the term referred to as an "Omniest."

As I discussed in the first part of my book, the connection between our spiritual health directly impacts and influences your physical and mental health's well-being. They are intrinsically linked. The simple act of belief has tremendous benefits in increasing your longevity, your physiological and psychological health.

Why is that? Generally, those who believe in a higher power have better relationships with more awareness of the importance of compassion and forgiveness. They typically handle challenging emotions and stress better. A more optimistic view helps them be psychologically resilient.

Believing is also accredited to better cardiovascular health, a decreased risk of depression, and stronger immune responses. Spiritual individuals tend to be more satisfied and content, leading to more fulfilling lives.

Some will rationalize reasoning with science or the placebo effect, which is fine; at least they believe in something. I prefer believing in something that gives me excitement, optimism, hope, and miracles.

Our mere existence is miraculous. The extraordinary coincidences that allow Earth to support life are almost unbelievable.

For starters, Earth is in perfect proximity from the sun with a magnetic field that protects us from harmful radiation. Then, it is just the right size to have an optimal atmosphere that protects and insulates it, creating an ideal temperature. It naturally just orbits an imaginary line in space consistently.

More importantly, it's perfectly unique, tilted axis provides us with seasons and prevents temperature extremes. The axis also provides the appropriate amount of daylight in a twenty-four-hour period. The combination of energy resources and nutrient-rich chemicals, such as water and carbon, produce minerals that allow the formation of life.

Additionally, the moon stabilizes the axis's spin and direction, creating this ideal climate to sustain life. We are also perfectly positioned to be protected from incoming debris from our wonderful neighbor, Jupiter, that mostly sucks up any potential harmful objects from colliding into us.

These, and other factors, make our existence more than phenomenal.

In our entire galaxy, with over 300 billion stars, Earth is the only planet that is fully inhabitable.

Our existence on the Earth is miraculous, for the Earth itself is miraculous, but more importantly, the human body is a miracle in itself. Ponder, just for a second, the human body and its capabilities.

Your heart does massive work while you are fast asleep. Your body regenerates cells. It dispenses vital nutrients where needed so your body can function. It recovers, replenishes, and restores itself without any conscious effort from you. Our bodies are miracles.

You will never convince me that our planet and our bodies are not a creation from a higher power.

As you start to become aware of everything around you, it's very hard to not see the magic that transpires every day in so many ways. "I could go through this day oblivious to the miracles all around me or I could tune in and 'enjoy.'"[18]

Be open to connecting. If you feel lost, start asking for signs. You will soon begin to realize that you are being heard. You will also discover that within you lie the answers.

When I am struggling to control my fear, doubts, or anxiety, I call on a higher power to help me. Believing doesn't mean you won't experience negative emotions; it just means you know that you don't have to go through it alone. I cannot tell you how often I look up from my day with a smile full of gratitude knowing I just witnessed God's work. I know undoubtedly, a higher power has helped me in specific situations.

However, you have to do your part. The combination of your best effort and a little "luck" will produce desirable outcomes. Do all that you can do, and then you can, like a balloon, just let it go.

There is incredible joy found when letting it go and leaving it to a higher power. The power is working with you if you let it. Believing is beautiful, and doubt is dreadful!

You can start connecting to your spiritual side with small steps just like I did:

1) Be open to a new journey.
2) Explore different concepts and beliefs. Learn new practices and techniques. Try a few to determine what you are comfortable with.
3) Incorporate small acts and rituals into your daily routine. In the morning, it will be in your consciousness throughout the day; and in the evening, it will rest in your subconscious as you sleep. Either way, both are great.
4) Be consistent in taking the time to practice and connect. You will become more present as you begin to invest in your spiritual self.

21

ABUNDANCE

"Gratitude is like a magnet; the more grateful you are, the more you will receive to be grateful for."—Lyanla Vanzant

Whatever your spiritual source, connecting with your spiritual side brings more spiritual abundance. This is more than a material abundance and has nothing to do with wealth, possessions, or fame. This type of abundance means tapping into your deepest, inner self while allowing your higher power to provide for your needs.

To achieve that, you need to believe that abundance and prosperity are possible; think positively about your present and future state, and adopt an abundance mentality.

Essentially, you must tap into the power of your mind and beliefs to achieve your dreams, drawing on whatever spiritual source you use—God, the universe, etc.

GRATITUDE

In order to connect with your deeper self and achieve spiritual abundance, you need to practice being grateful. Gratitude is important because it acknowledges all the good. It generates positive and optimistic feelings.

If you allow yourself to get down and focus on what you do not have, it is easy to forget everything you do have.

Since spiritual abundance requires you to think positively about your present state, gratitude helps you achieve that as gratitude changes the lens in which we view the world. Gratitude allows us to really see and focus on the beauty already present in our world.

It is the result of the abundance mentality, since focusing on what you have helps you recognize your abundance. It magnifies things that have gone unnoticed, felt monotonous, or become routine, that, quite frankly, you take for granted.

Not only does it magnify things, but it also makes simple things more special and good because it is like a new discovery. You will have a new excitement because you now appreciate these things in a new way.

Additionally, gratitude changes the way we respond to people and situations. Grateful people are more likely to deal with people in a more kind, generous, and compassionate way.

Gratitude will keep you patient on your journey. On your way to achieve your goals, the challenges can be exceedingly difficult. You will have good days and bad days. On your bad days, it will be hard not to get down. If you do, that is okay, as long as you don't stay there. Practicing gratitude consistently will pull you out of your dark headspace much quicker.

Most importantly, I think gratitude provides you with hope for a better future. Because we are already aware of what currently exists, we see potential in even more to come. It gives us a better perspective, makes us more aware, provides appreciation, and generates excitement.

I think gratitude journaling is particularly important as it keeps things in perspective. You should do it daily. I have found that right before bed is a good time. I wake up the next day ready to observe the things I can report back to my journal that evening.

Just three things. It doesn't even have to be achievements or accomplishments. Your list can be small and simple, such as the smell of the laundry or the wind in your hair. Try listing new things every time.

Then, once a month, I strongly suggest you reflect on what you have been able to accomplish and what you are most proud of. It might just be the gratitude you've generated and the happiness it gives you.

Reflection will give you a sense of renewal and revitalize you to keep moving forward as you continue to make progress and improve.

AFFIRMATIONS

Years ago, I heard affirmations can help you achieve future abundance. By simply saying your desires out loud and really visualizing your words, your desires manifest into reality.

I kept brushing that concept off until I decided to give it a try. I was astonished by how much they actually work.

How is that even possible? Is it God, the universe? Call it what you will. I have no idea how, but they have worked for me and many others. Go ahead, eye roll. I did it plenty of times before I tried. I can only encourage you to try it with the argument, what have you got to lose?

Affirmations go along with the law of attraction principles. It simply means, positive will attract positive, and vice versa, negative will attract negative. By creating and surrounding yourself with the right energy, you will attract what you desire.

Affirmations help you keep your intention in the forefront of your mind. You say them with conviction, and your belief in the possibilities will help shift your mind, ideas, actions, and overall being.

I am not going to lie; affirmations are uncomfortable at first. You are shouting thoughts out loud that are not necessarily how you feel. But it is important to keep practicing putting out your intentions and desire until, not only do you begin to feel them, but you also believe they are possible.

Now, will they alone produce results? Absolutely not, but they do bring a sense of awareness to opportunities and advantages that would have otherwise gone left unnoticed.

You should do them every day, even twice a day, perhaps morning and night. If you say them before bed, it will instill them in your subconscious.

When you say affirmations, they must be stated as true statements that are already happening. Thus, they begin with, *"I am,"* not *"I will."* The phrase, *"I am,"* implies it is available, present, and already happening. The idea is simply to experience the feeling as if your desire is already here. Tapping into the emotion is necessary with affirmations because the more you feel it, the more real it becomes. If it is real, then you can obtain it.

If you want to open your new business, an affirmation would not be, "I will open up a business this year and be very successful." It would be, "I am a successful entrepreneur living my dream."

Here are a few examples of my recent affirmations which align with my goals and vision for myself:

I AM GROWING AND IMPROVING EVERY DAY.
I AM AN AMAZING MOTHER AND A WONDERFUL WIFE.
I TAKE ACTION AND CURE MY FEARS.
I HAVE 50 NEW CLIENTS.
I AM KIND, CARING, LOVING, AND COMPASSIONATE.
I AM A BEST-SELLING AUTHOR WHO HELPS COUNTLESS
    PEOPLE.

There are plenty of resources on affirmations and meditation, so feel free to do more research.

SCARCITY MENTALITY VS. ABUNDANCE MENTALITY

I first heard about this concept in Steven R. Covey's, *The Seven Habits of Highly Effective People,* and I felt a little uncomfortable. I was guilty of some behaviors in the scarcity mentality. It was eye-opening.

Until you fully develop your self-esteem, self-worth, and confidence, you will keep falling back into the scarcity mentality.

People tend to think in two very distinct ways: the negative, scarcity thinking and the positive, abundance belief. These mentalities determine the way you see yourself, others, and your overall view of the world. One will keep your mind enslaved, while the other one will set it free.

A scarcity mindset has a very pessimistic outlook. These individuals are small-minded, feel a sense of entitlement, and assume the victim mentality. They relinquish any power of control.

Scarcity mindset beliefs:

- I am never at fault.
- My life circumstances have been very unfair.
- Certain people are a certain way.
- Life has been, and always will be, hard. There is no changing it.

- Things are always working against me.
- There is never enough, so I do not share.

Scarcity mindset feelings:

- Not happy and resentful when others experience success.
- Afraid of taking risks.
- Fear competition.

For example, someone with this mentality would think, *I have anger issues, and I cannot help it.*

An abundance mentality, as I mentioned, is the complete opposite. These individuals have an extremely optimistic view. The glass is always half full in their mind. They find opportunities because when there is not one, they make one.

Abundance mindset beliefs:

- Dream big.
- I have the power to dictate my future.
- I should share compliments.
- Competition strengthens my skills.
- Challenges should be embraced.
- If one door closes, another door or window will open.
- There is plenty to go around.
- My time will come.
- The more I give, the more I get.
- I need to be willing to take risks and not fear failure.
- It is important to help others.

Abundance mindset feelings:

- Compassionate
- Fulfilled

The abundance mentality will carry you far in your journey. It is about hope in the unknown and the acceptance and gratitude throughout.

GRACEFULLY LETTING GO

Letting go of beliefs, habits, relationships, situations, and security can be terrifying. You have to be audacious in order to let go of the familiar and discover what awaits you. There are no guarantees, but there are possibilities.

When you evolve, you have to change. It requires you to let go of who you think you are in order to become who you are meant to be!

CONCLUSION

As you connect with your deeper self and bring spiritual abundance into your life, you need to remember to practice gratitude, adopt an abundance mindset, and use affirmations. Gratitude will shift your perspective and grant you permission to see the world exactly as it is. It allows you to become more present and more positive about your surroundings. Practice gratitude daily. Remember to write at least three things you are grateful for in a gratitude journal every day.

Try affirmations for just one month. Really do so with optimistic intentions. See what happens. You have got nothing to lose.

Start applying the abundance mentality. Be aware of the scarcity thinkers around you. The greater your ability to recognize the scarcity thoughts in your mind or the people who think this way, the easier you can justify why they are toxic and should be avoided.

Let go of things that do not serve you. Whether it is worry, stress, or fear, these carry tremendous weight.

You must let go of things you outgrow.

Never believe you are unworthy of great things. In fact, throughout your journey, you will have to give up the good for the great. You are much more deserving than you think.

22

TURN ON THE LIGHT

*"And if the whole wide world stops singing and all the
stars go dark, I'll keep the light on in my soul, and keep
a bluebird in my heart." —Miranda Lambert*

Once you have connected with your spiritual side, you will find your intuition and ability to hope will increase. Use your intuition, always have hope, and you will fulfill your plan to adopt an audacious mindset.

INTUITION

*"What the mind holds is experience. What the soul
holds is knowledge."—Neale Donald Walsch*

Your intuition is of great value and incredible. It is a sense that you really ought to home in on, as it will be the voice that guides you. Your intuition is never wrong.

Your outside voices or past experiences will attempt to silence this intuition, which is the truth about what is yours, what you can have, choices you need to make, paths you need to follow, and the ideas and things you need to let go of.

Do not listen to that self-doubt. Follow the initial ideas that pop into your mind, gut, or even your heart. They are telling you something, so listen to them and see where it leads you.

So many people hesitate and disregard this sense that they eventually suppress it. To revive and cultivate your intuition, you need to take time to self-reflect. Journaling is a great tool to capture your thoughts, emotions, and ideas. Reflect on those previous journal entries to notice patterns that can help you become more aware. Sit in silence, meditate, or just be at one with yourself a few minutes a day to gather your thoughts.

Once you learn how to tap into your inner being, you can begin to recognize yourself and become aware of what is happening around you more clearly. You will have a better understanding of your motivations, enthusiasm, passion, strengths, and challenges. My intuition has been a constant force in my life. I have used it with every major decision and situation in my life. To be honest, without very much contemplation either. If I ponder too long and ignore that initial voice, my emotions, and other factors try and complicate what I already know the answer to be.

When I am lost, I pray and find the voice within me. It is one of my greatest assets and strengths. My intuition is what guides me to leave bad, or even good situations to pursue better ones. I act first and hope second.

It was what guided me to Detroit for a boy I hardly knew, who was in a completely different point in his life than me, with the hope it would all work out.

My intuition also made me quit my stable job for an industry in which I had no experience, knowledge, or skills.

It pushed me in the direction of this book, even though English was my worst subject in school. I never wanted to be an author, and I did not have the slightest clue on how to write a book, yet I cannot help but be excited because I know that I am supposed to do this.

Always take that risk when it can better you, your situation, or your life. "Do not fear the unknown. The unknown is where the rest of you resides. The only thing you will discover there is more of yourself. There's nothing to be afraid of."[19]

When your inner voice tells you something consistently enough, you better listen. It is doing so for a reason. Otherwise, you risk forsaking something that is your destiny.

HOPE

"No matter what sort of difficulties, how painful experience is, if we lose our hope, that's our real disaster." —The Dalai Lama.

All throughout my life, I have struggled with an autoimmune disease. Signs of it come and go. I never know what is going to bring it on, how it's going to present itself, or how long it is going to last.

It first made its appearance when I was about thirteen. I was diagnosed with eczema. My body was covered for a few weeks with big red circle patches. What started with a few patches quickly grew to cover my entire body, reaching up to my neck toward my face. When I finally got treated, they dissolved until they made an appearance later in my adult years.

Then, I developed Bell's palsy right after the delivery of my daughter. It is when one side of your face goes completely paralyzed. It typically happens in older folks after a stroke. I was told it was caused by a virus, but it can be associated with pregnancy.

I had just become a mother for the very first time, and I was also confronted with facial paralysis. I didn't want to take pictures because one side of my mouth was unable to smile. I had to sleep with a patch because I couldn't close my one eye. However, it was a new challenge I had to deal with.

Slight signs of improvement started at two weeks, and after three weeks, it was completely gone.

The doctor told me I was at a greater risk of developing Bell's palsy for any future pregnancies. I was also told that drafts of cold wind to your face have been known to trigger Bell's palsy as well.

Needless to say, I never let it deter me from having my baby boy, or from going skiing with my family. My faith and hope are stronger than my fear.

The scariest experience I have had so far with my autoimmune disease, which really has no distinct explanation or cure, was when I was hospitalized. Even after I was released, they had no answers for the attack that put me there.

It happened on a Sunday when we were out of town. I told my husband how much my body hurt and how I could barely move. He kept telling me it was the flu because he always gets very achy.

I tried to tell him this was different. My joints started swelling, and I had to be helped to the car because I physically could not do it on my own.

Once we arrived home, I had to lay in bed; but my hands, ankles, and wrists were so swollen, and my pain had become so unbearable, that I made my husband take me to the emergency room immediately.

When we arrived at the hospital, I had to be assisted by a wheelchair, and I was crying because of the immense pain I was feeling. They hydrated me, hooked me up to an IV, and ran many different tests.

Lyme disease, lupus, you name it. In the end, after a few hours of treatment, I was a lot better. They concluded it was an autoimmune disease but provided no other details.

The only explanation was that it was some type of hyper immune response where a virus had presented itself, and my body attacked my joints and my nerves.

I have no idea what "viruses" are going to cause my body to behave this way. I have no idea when, where, what, how, and why this will occur. I cannot prepare, and I don't know what to avoid. It is so far out of my control that it would be impossible to think that I could. All I can do is let go of this burden that could weigh me down and release it.

"Sometimes all you can do is accept there's not much you can do. And sometimes all you can control is how well you let go of control."[20]

A belief in a higher power will help you breed hope. It is a virtue born from optimism, with a belief for better circumstances and a better future. Living with hope is the healthiest and happiest way. Hope must be gained when you lose control. It will serve as your strength.

1) First, start believing in a higher power. You are not alone.
2) Focus on what you can control. Implement and place a high value on daily rituals, affirmations, gratitude, prayers, and faith. When you do so, you will naturally have hope.
3) Remember, you are blessed beyond measure. Trust the plan!

CONCLUSION

Your intuition is like that sixth sense that allows you to be so aware that you can feel. It is a sense within all of us that remains largely untapped. It will be your intuition that will guide you. It will connect dots for you and allow you to be your true, authentic self.

Hope is the reason I survived my childhood and found success.

Hope is the reason I pursue risks, and it is the reason I have an optimistic belief about the future. It is what gives me the audacity to push a little further, reach a little higher, and discover a little more. It can do the same for you.

The only thing you ever need to forever cling to is hope. Without it, all else is lost.

CONCLUSION
BE UNAPOLOGETICALLY AUDACIOUS

When you achieve an audacious mindset, you will recognize and exercise the power and authority within yourself. It is the discovery, decision, and development of exactly what you want to do and who you want to be. It is the understanding that you are in complete control of your life. It is about adapting, mastering, and organizing yourself and your environment to pursue your desires.

Here are the seven intertwined concepts recapped:

1. Master your mind: If you cannot master yourself, your attitude, your actions, your life, or your circumstances, the rest will be of little use. You will limit yourself if you live by the limitations you allow in your mind. It will take time to build trust within yourself. However, you can do this and demand more for yourself by reflecting on your values, creating a clear vision, and setting goals, habits, and rituals to help you meet that vision. These will lead to fulfillment.

2. Self-respect: You are worthy of what you want. Self-respect validates the authority you hold over your life. Make sure to establish the boundaries, discipline, and accountability you deserve. Honor yourself by being authentic. Look at who is in your inner circle, and only allow in those who will help you foster your self-respect.

3. Confidence: Acknowledge and accept your perceived strengths and weaknesses because both are valuable. To gain the needed confidence, let go of negative feelings toward others, such as jealousy, comparisons, and judgment. Be confident that your time will come. Let go of perfectionism and silence your inner critic. Confidence will be gained by pushing past your comfort zone continuously. Nourish your body, strengthen your mind, and practice confident acts.

4. Fight: Fight to awaken the power to change within you. When you decide to start living up to your potential, you activate that power. If you do not take the initiative, your power will lie dormant and be unknown.

Operate with a warrior mentality. Have the steadfast determination and willpower to keep rising every time you fall. You are strong enough to fight and succeed at whatever it is you want.

5. Passion: Discover what you're passionate about and use that enthusiasm to motivate you. Enthusiasm will keep you energized and propel you ahead. Your passion will help you reject your fears. It will keep you focused, and it will not allow you to settle for less. Passion will help you pursue your purpose with full dedication.

6. Courage: The key part of courage is action. You must take actions, bold or otherwise, to diminish your fears. Hesitation only hinders you. Remember to doubt your doubts before you doubt your abilities. When you aren't willing to risk anything, you risk everything. Fear will try to hold you back and diminish what you can become. An audacious mindset will give you the fortitude to keep pursuit.

7. Faith: Connect to your spiritual side in whatever form that may be, so you find your deeper self and clear center.

This will come through practicing awareness, gratitude, abundance, and acceptance. This will allow you to live a life full of fun, joy, love, passion, and peace. Optimism, faith, and hope will serve as your greatest assets to keep daring and believing that the chances you take will grant you all that you desire.

An audacious mindset values freedom. Free from self-defeating beliefs, free from worry, free from doubts, free from judgments, free to be bold, and free to take risks. The freedom to explore endless possibilities and your limitless potential.

Your journey is determined by you. This is your life, and you get to make up the rules.

NOTES

Section 1

[1] Confucius, "Thoughts On The Business Of Life," quoted in "Thoughts on the Business of Life," Forbes Quotes, accessed February 11, 2021, https://www.forbes.com/quotes/1913/.

[2] Louis Brandeis, "What Publicity Can Do," *Harper's Weekly* (1913), quoted in WIST, last modified January 8, 2011, https://wist.info/brandeis-louis/5564/.

Chapter 7

[3] Steven Furtick, Twitter, https://twitter.com/stevenfurtick/status/679819137 46444288?lang=en.

Chapter 8

[4] Carolyn Gregoire, "Fourteen Signs Your Perfectionism Has Gotten Out of Control," *Huffington Post*, last updated December 6, 2017, https://www.huffpost.com/entry/why-perfectionism-is-ruin_n_4212069.

Chapter 9

[5] "Confidence," *Oxford Dictionary*, Lexico, May 5, 2020, accessed February 11, 2021, https://www.lexico.com/en/definition/confidence

[6] Ben Franklin, quoted in Justin Bryant, "An Investment in Knowledge Pays the Best Interest," Self Made Success, June 10, 2016, https://selfmadesuccess.com/investment-knowledge-pays-best-interest/.

[7] College Foundation of North Carolina, "Self-confidence: A Key to Success," CFNC.org, 2016. https://www1.cfnc.org/Home/Article.

aspx?articleId=TKZjBonzsuebU8XAP2BPAXEAiXAP2FPAX11wXAP3D-
PAXXAP3DPAX&level=3XAP2FPAX6J7I3kztATGuYyXAP2BPAXDahIQX-
AP3DPAXXAP3DPAX.

Chapter 10

8   Joyce Meyer, quoted in Pass It On, accessed February 15, 2021, https://www.pas-siton.com/inspirational-quotes/7725-patience-is-not-simply-the-ability-to-wait.

9   Prasad Mahes, "The Power of the Pause," World Happiness Summit, January 8, 2019, https://www.happinesssummit.world/index.php/2019/01/08/the-power-of-the-pause/.

10   Unknown.

Chapter 11

11   Yip Hurburg, *Over The Rainbow,* written for the Wizard of Oz, 1938.

12   PK, "Average Income by State plus Median, Top 1%, and All Income Percentiles in 2020. Median Individual Income by State," DQYDJ, accessed February 11, 2021, https://dqydj.com/average-income-by-state-median-top-percentiles/.

13   Jim Rohn, "10 Unforgettable Quotes by Jim Rohn," Success, September 17, 2019, https://www.success.com/10-unforgettable-quotes-by-jim-rohn/.

14   Gloria Gaither, *Five minutes in the Morning,* (New York: Simon & Shuster, 2006), 30.

Chapter 14

15   Nirandhi Gowthaman, "12 Inspirational Quotes by Eleanor Roosevelt to Help You Navigate Life," HerStory, Your Story, September 8, 2019, https://yourstory.com/herstory/2019/09/inspirational-quotes-eleanor-roosevelt-navigate-life.

Chapter 15

16   Jeb Blount, *Fanatical Prospecting*, (Hoboken: John Wiley & Sons, 2015), 192.

Chapter 17

[17] Roosevelt, Franklin D. (Franklin Delano), 1882-1945. Franklin D. Roosevelt's Inaugural Address of 1933. Washington, DC :National Archives and Records Administration, 1988.

Chapter 22

[18] Gloria Gaither, *"Five minutes in the Morning,"* (New York: Simon & Shuster, 2006), 51.

[19] Unknown.

[20] Lori Deschene, quoted in "The Quote Archive," Tiny Buddha, accessed February 11, 2021, https://tinybuddha.com/wisdom-quotes/sometimes-all-you-can-do-i s-accept-theres-not-much-you-can-do/.

ACKNOWLEDGMENTS

know without a doubt none of this would be possible without the grace of god. Thank you for all the signs, guidance, knowledge, insight, and wisdom you sprinkled throughout this journey.

To Chandler Bolt and the Self-Publishing School family, thank you for all your help, information, and resources. Your support helped me navigate unchartered territory with confidence.

To Jenna, Lauren, Stephanie, and Jessica, my wonderful childhood caretakers, thank you. Your friendships are what saved me in my youth. Thank you for your unconditional love, loyalty, and support at a time when I needed it the most. I will be forever grateful for you.

Brooke Lopez, who captured my cover photo, thanks. You and Lisa Ross find a way to make all my professional and personal photographs fabulous. Thank you for being the elite photographers, and more importantly, the type of friends that elevate me!

My parents, through it all, I love you. I know you were struggling, making mistakes, and learning as does every person and parent. Without those hardships, I would not be the strong independent woman I was meant to be, so thank you!

Beau, my better half, no amount of thanks would ever be enough. You always believed in me even when I struggled to believe in myself. Because of you, I know anything is possible. You are my biggest encourager and supporter. I will never be able to fully express the gratitude and appreciation I have for you. I love you and thank you so very much. You and our children are the greatest blessings I will ever know.

Lastly, Haydn and Broc, you motivate me to do better. You have given me a new perspective on life. You may not realize it, but you are teaching me everyday in new ways. Being your mama is my deepest treasure. Thank you so much!

ABOUT THE AUTHOR

Growing up, Heather faced abandonment and instability, leading to her making several reckless decisions. But after repeatedly getting knocked down, she learned to master the art of overcoming all odds and found success: marrying the man of her dreams, raising two children, and becoming a top 4% individual income earner in the entire U.S.

It was her audacious mindset that helped her achieve all this. She knows all too well that fortune favors the audacious and the tenacious.

In an effort to be a strong female mentor for her daughter, she wrote this book to inspire and guide all those young women who feel lost, or stuck, on their journey. By tapping into their unclaimed resource, their mind, they can access a freedom readily available. It is the freedom to achieve and exceed what they can conceive as long as they stop using their past, any setbacks, and obstacles as excuses. Heather stopped playing the victim and took the initiative to be a victor, and you can too.

Can You Help?

Thank You For Reading My Book!

I really appreciate all of your feedback, and I love hearing what you have to say.

I need your input to make the next version of this book and my future books better.

Please leave me an honest review on Amazon letting me know what you thought of the book.

Thanks so much!

All the Best,
Heather

Made in the USA
Las Vegas, NV
15 June 2021